HOW TO SURVIVE
IN A WORLD OF UNBELIEVERS

HOW TO SURVIVE
IN A WORLD OF UNBELIEVERS

Jesus' Words of Encouragement on the Night Before His Death

JOHN MACARTHUR

WORD PUBLISHING

NASHVILLE

A Thomas Nelson Company

HOW TO SURVIVE IN A WORLD OF UNBELIEVERS

Copyright © 2001 by John F. MacArthur, Jr.

All rights reserved.

Published by Word Publishing, a unit of Thomas Nelson, Inc.,
P. O. Box 141000, Nashville, Tennessee 37214.

No portion of this book may be reproduced in any form
without the written permission of the copyright owner,
except for brief excerpts quoted in critical reviews.

All Scripture quotations in this book, except those noted otherwise, are
from the New King James Version, © 1984 by Thomas Nelson, Inc.

Quotations marked NASB are from the New American Standard Bible,
© 1960, 1962, 1963, 1968, 1971, 1972, 1973, 1975, 1977, 1988, and
1995 by The Lockman Foundation, and are used by permission.

Quotations marked NIV are from
The Holy Bible: New International Version.
© Copyright 1973, 1978, 1984 by the International Bible Society.
All rights reserved. Used by permission of Zondervan Bible Publishers.

Quotations marked KJV are from the King James Version of the Bible.

ISBN 0-8499-5556-4

Printed in the United States of America

01 02 03 04 05 PHX 6 5 4 3 2 1

CONTENTS

INTRODUCTION

WITHOUT QUESTION, SOME OF THE MOST POIGNANT, POWERFUL teaching in Jesus' entire earthly ministry took place on the last evening He spent with His disciples before He was crucified. The occasion was the Passover meal, commonly known as the Last Supper. Jesus' earthly ministry to the masses had just ended and He had turned the focus of His teaching time uniquely on the apostles (John 13–16). That ministry occurred in a brief period of hours, just before He was arrested and led away for trial, and in one place, the upper room.

During those hours, Jesus gave His disciples—and, consequently, all believers throughout history—His last will and testament. It is the inheritance of every believer in Christ. It will be our privilege to look into those words of encouragement and challenge in *How to Survive in a World of Unbelievers*. But we will only scratch the surface of a portion of the rich promise contained in just three chapters of our Lord's final discourse. You will easily see that a lifetime of study still might not plumb the depths of all that He taught us about living for Him in an unbelieving world. Here is a preview of the rich truths we'll study in John 13–16:

Christ gave proof of His love. "Jesus . . . rose from supper and laid aside His garments, took a towel and girded Himself. After that, He poured water into a basin and began to wash the disciples' feet, and to wipe them with the towel with which He was girded" (John 13:3–5). Later, Peter and the rest of the disciples would know Christ's love through His atoning death. But in the upper room they saw a glimpse of it through Jesus' washing of their feet.

Jesus gave the hope of heaven. "'Let not your heart be troubled; you believe in God, believe also in Me. In My Father's house are many mansions; if it were not so, I would have told you. I go to prepare a place for you. And if I go and prepare a place for you, I will come again and receive you to Myself; that where I am, there you may be also'" (14:1–3). In those days in Israel, when a son married, a new apartment was added onto the father's house. Generation after generation of the extended family lived together in one home. That is how heaven is. We are all to be in the Father's house. Jesus is preparing our rooms.

Our Lord gave us the guarantee of power. "'Most assuredly, I say to you, he who believes in Me, the works that I do he will do also; and greater works than these he will do, because I go to My Father'" (14:12). Jesus did not mean the disciples would do works that were greater than His in quality or type, but that they would do works that were greater in extent. During Christ's ministry on earth He faced mostly rejection, and He never left the tiny land of Palestine. But on the day of Pentecost, the Spirit of God came, and the apostles started preaching and revolutionized Jerusalem. Later, when persecution came to the Christians in Jerusalem, they scattered throughout Samaria and Judea, preaching the gospel as they went. Then the Apostle Paul and his associates spread the gospel to many more lands. That process is still going on today.

Jesus gave the assurance of supply. "'And whatever you ask in My name, that will I do, that the Father may be glorified in the Son. If you ask anything in My name, I will do it'" (14:13–14). To pray in His name is to bring requests before God that are consistent with who He is. Prayer is not merely for us to satisfy our selfish desires, and it is not to dissuade God from doing what He is going to do anyway. Prayer is to give God the opportunity to show Himself so that we can praise Him for what He is doing.

Our Savior gave the gift of the Spirit. "'And I will pray the Father, and He will give you another Helper, that He may abide with you forever—the Spirit of truth'" (14:16–17a). Jesus promised a supernatural Helper, or Comforter, of the exact same kind as He. This Comforter is the Holy Spirit, the Spirit of Christ. He lives within Christ's disciples, not just near them. He empowers them and convicts those to whom they preach. His ministry is to "'convict the world of sin . . . because they do not believe in Me; of righteousness, because I go to my Father and you see Me no more; of judgment, because the ruler of this world is judged'" (16:8–11).

The Master gave every genuine follower the possession of divine truth, the Word of God. "'But the Helper, the Holy Spirit, whom the Father will send in My name, He will teach you all things, and bring to your remembrance all things that I said to you'" (14:26). This promise had a primary application to the writers of the New Testament, the apostolic preachers in the early era of the church. It was a promise of verbal inspiration. The Holy Spirit would bring to their remembrance all that Jesus had taught them, and He would give them further teaching through the years as they served Him. The Bible is accurate, for the Holy Spirit never lies. There is no lie in Him; He is the "Spirit of truth" (14:17; 15:26; 16:13).

Furthermore, *He promised the gift of peace.* "'Peace I leave with you, My peace I give to you; not as the world gives do I give to you. Let not your heart be troubled, neither let it be afraid'" (14:27). One kind of peace in Scripture is peace *with* God. That is the objective peace of relationship with Him. But there is also the subjective peace of tranquillity of mind, the peace *of* God. "The Lord is at hand," Paul writes in Philippians 4:5. But that is not a reference to the second coming. It is a reference to the presence of the Lord in our lives today. Because He is at hand, we should be "anxious for nothing" (v. 6).

He promised the blessing of spiritual fruit. "'I am the vine, you are the branches. He who abides in Me, and I in him, bears much fruit; for without Me you can do nothing'" (John 15:5). Fruit is the product of a life that has continuing vitality. It lives beyond us; it is something we reproduce. Christians are part of a product that will go throughout eternity like ripples in an everlasting pond. We have lives that will reverberate through all the corridors of heaven forever and ever.

In a more sobering vein, *Christ also promised the pain of persecution.* "'If the world hates you, you know that it hated Me before it hated you. If you were of the world, the world would love its own. Yet because you are not of the world, but I chose you out of the world, therefore the world hates you'" (15:18–19). The servant is not greater than his Lord. The world hates and rejects the message of sin. Christ unmasks the world and reveals its sin. So the world hates Him, and it hates us. Jesus warned His disciples, "'These things I have spoken to you, that you should not be made to stumble'" (16:1).

Finally, *He promised true joy.* "'These things I have spoken to you, that My joy may remain in you, and that your joy may be full'" (15:11). Joy is the result of everything Jesus has said, everything He has given us. A woman has agony when she is in labor, but when she gives birth to a child, she remembers her pain no more. Believers will have sorrow and painful circumstances, but out of those very circumstances will come the greatest joy. Jesus says, "'I will see you again and your heart will rejoice, and your joy no one will take from you'" (16:22b).

My prayer in offering this book is that those of you who know Jesus Christ as Lord and Savior will grow in your understanding of the riches that are yours because of His love for you. And if you do not know Him, may the Lord convict you of your need to surrender completely to Him.

As we study these chapters together, may the Spirit of God impress on each of you the importance of giving your all to Him who freely gave His all for you.

ONE

THE HUMILITY OF LOVE

W^E LIVE IN A VERY PROUD AND EGOTISTICAL GENERATION. People now consider it acceptable and even normal for others to promote themselves, praise themselves, and put themselves first. Many consider pride a virtue. On the other hand, many people view humility as a weakness. Everyone, it seems, is screaming for his or her own rights and seeking to be recognized as someone important.

The preoccupation with self-esteem, self-love, and self-glory is destroying the very foundations upon which our society is built. No culture can survive pride run rampant, for all of society depends on relationships. When people are committed first of all to themselves, relationships disintegrate. And that is just what is happening in our culture, as friendships, marriages, and families fall apart.

Sadly, the preoccupation with self has found its way into the church. Perhaps the fastest growing phenomenon in modern Christianity is the emphasis on pride, self-esteem, self-image, self-fulfillment, and other manifestations of selfism. Out of it is emerging a new religion of self-centeredness, pride—even arrogance. Voices from every part of the theological spectrum call us to join the self-esteem cult.

Scripture is clear, however, that selfism has no place in Christian

1

theology. Jesus repeatedly taught against pride, and with His life and teaching He constantly exalted the virtue of humility. Nowhere is that more clear than in John 13.

"HE LOVED THEM TO THE END"

Chapter 13 marks a turning point in John's gospel and the ministry of Jesus Christ. Jesus' public ministry to the people of Israel had run its course and ended in their complete and final rejection of Him as Messiah. On the first day of the week, Jesus had entered Jerusalem in triumph to the enthusiastic shouts of the people. Yet they never truly understood His ministry and His message. The Passover season had arrived, and by Friday He would be utterly rejected and then executed. God, however, would turn that execution into the great and final sacrifice for sin, and Jesus would die as the true Passover Lamb.

He had come to His own people, the Jews, "and His own did not receive Him" (John 1:11). So He had turned away from His public ministry to the intimate fellowship of His disciples.

Now it was the day before Jesus' death, and rather than being preoccupied with thoughts of His death, sin-bearing, and glorification, He was totally consumed with His love for the disciples. Although He knew He would soon go to the cross to die for the sins of the world, Jesus was still concerned with the needs of twelve men. His love was never and is never impersonal—that's the mystery of it.

In what were literally the last hours before His death, Jesus kept showing the disciples His love over and over. John relates this graphic demonstration of it:

Now before the Feast of the Passover, when Jesus knew that His hour had come that He should depart from this world to the Father, having loved His own who were in the world, He loved them to the end.

And supper being ended, the devil having already put it into the heart of Judas Iscariot, Simon's son, to betray him, Jesus, knowing that the Father had given all things into His hands, and that He had come from God and was going to God, rose from supper and laid aside His garments, took a towel and girded Himself. After that, He poured water into a basin and began to wash the disciples' feet, and to wipe them with the towel with which He was girded. Then He came to Simon Peter. And Peter said to Him, "Lord, are You washing my feet?"

Jesus answered and said to him, "What I am doing you do not understand now, but you will know after this."

Peter said to Him, "You shall never wash my feet!"

Jesus answered him, "If I do not wash you, you have no part with Me."

Simon Peter said to Him, "Lord, not my feet only, but also my hands and my head."

Jesus said to him, "He who is bathed needs only to wash his feet, but is completely clean; and you are clean, but not all of you." For He knew who would betray Him; therefore He said, "You are not all clean."

So when He had washed their feet, taken His garments, and sat down again, He said to them, "Do you know what I have done to you? You call Me Teacher and Lord, and you say well, for so I am. If I then, your Lord and Teacher, have washed your feet, you also ought to wash one another's feet. For I have given you an example, that you should do as I have done to you. Most assuredly, I say to you, a servant is not greater than his master; nor is he who is sent greater than he who sent him. If you know these things, blessed are you if you do them." (John 13:1–17)

It is very likely that Jesus and the disciples had been hiding at Bethany during this final week before the crucifixion. Having come from there (or from anywhere near Jerusalem), they would have had to travel on extremely dirty roads. Naturally, by the time they arrived, their feet were covered with dust from the road.

Everyone in that culture faced the same problem. Sandals did little to keep dirt off the feet, and the roads were either a thick layer of dust or deep masses of mud. At the entrance to every Jewish home was a large pot of water to wash dirty feet. Normally, foot washing was the duty of the lowliest slave. When guests came, he had to go to the door and wash their feet—not a pleasant task. In fact, washing feet was probably his most abject duty, and only slaves performed it for others. Even the disciples of rabbis were not to wash the feet of their masters— that was uniquely the task of a slave.

As Jesus and His disciples all arrived in the upper room, they did not meet a servant who would wash their feet. Only days before, Jesus had said to the twelve, "Whoever desires to become great among you, let him be your servant. And whoever desires to be first among you, let him be your slave" (Matt. 20:26–27). If they had given mind and heart to His teaching, one of the twelve would have washed the others' feet, or they would have mutually shared the task. It could have been a beautiful thing, but because of their selfishness it never occurred to them. A parallel passage in Luke 22 gives us an idea just how selfish they were and what they were thinking about that evening:

> Now there was also a dispute among them, as to which of them should be considered the greatest. And He said to them, "The kings of the Gentiles exercise lordship over them, and those who exercise authority over them are called 'benefactors.' But not so among you; on the contrary, he who is the greatest among you, let him be as the younger, and he who governs as he who serves." (vv. 24–26)

What a sad scene that was! They were bickering about who was the greatest. And in an argument about who was the greatest, no one was going to get down on the ground and wash feet. The basin was there, the towel was there, and everything was ready. But no one moved to wash the others' feet.

If anyone in that room should have been thinking about the glory that would be his in the kingdom, it was Jesus. John 13:1 says that

Jesus knew His hour was come. He was on a divine time schedule, and He knew He was going to be with the Father. He was very conscious of the fact that He soon would be glorified: "Jesus, knowing that the Father had given all things into His hands, and that He had come from God and was going to God" (v. 3). But instead of being concerned with His glory, and in spite the disciples' selfishness, He was totally conscious of clearly revealing His personal love to the twelve that they might be secure in it.

Verse 1 says, "Having loved His own who were in the world, He loved them to the end." "To the end" in the Greek is *eis telos,* which means He loved them "to perfection." He loved them to the uttermost. He loved them with total fullness of love. That is the nature of Christ's love, and He showed it repeatedly—even in His death. When He was arrested, He arranged that the disciples would not be arrested. While He was on the cross, He made sure that John would care for His mother Mary in the years to come. He reached out to a dying thief and saved him. It is amazing that in those last hours of carrying the sins of the world, in the midst of all the pain and suffering He was bearing, He was conscious of that one would-be disciple hanging next to Him. He loves utterly, absolutely, to perfection, totally, completely, without reservation. At the moment when most men would have been wholly concerned with self, He selflessly humbled Himself to meet the needs of others. Genuine love is like that.

And here is the great lesson of this whole account: Only absolute humility can generate absolute love. It is the nature of love to be selfless, giving. In 1 Corinthians 13:5, Paul wrote that love "does not seek its own." In fact, to distill all the truth of 1 Corinthians 13 into one statement, we might say that the greatest virtue of love is its humility, for it is the humility of love that proves it and makes it visible.

Christ's love and His humility are inseparable. He could not have been so consumed with a passion for serving others, if He had been primarily concerned with Himself.

"LOVE . . . IN DEED AND IN TRUTH"

How could anyone reject that kind of love? People do it all the time. Judas did. "And supper being ended, the devil having already put it into the heart of Judas Iscariot, Simon's son, to betray him" (John 13:2). Do you see the tragedy of Judas? He was constantly basking in the light, yet living in darkness; experiencing the love of Christ, yet hating Him at the same time.

The contrast between Jesus and Judas is striking. And perhaps that is the very reason the Holy Spirit included verse 2 in this passage. Set against the backdrop of Judas' hatred, Jesus' love shines even brighter. We can better understand its magnitude when we understand that in the heart of Judas was the blackest kind of hatred and rejection. The words of love by which Jesus gradually drew the hearts of the other disciples to Himself only pushed Judas further and further away. The teaching by which He uplifted the souls of the other disciples just seemed to drive a stake into the heart of Judas. And everything that Jesus said in terms of love must have become like chafing shackles to Judas. From his fettered greed and his disappointed ambition began to spring jealousy, spite, and hatred—and now he was ready to destroy Christ, if need be.

But the more people hated Jesus and desired to hurt Him, the more it seemed He manifested love to them. From a human standpoint, it would be easy to understand if Jesus had reacted with resentment or bitterness. But all Jesus had was love—He even met the greatest injury with supreme love. In a little while He would be kneeling at the feet of Judas, washing them.

Jesus waited until everyone was seated and supper was served. Then, in an unforgettable act of humility that must have stunned the disciples, "[Jesus] rose from supper and laid aside His garments, took a towel and girded Himself. After that, He poured water into a basin and began to wash the disciples' feet, and to wipe them with the towel with which He was girded" (John 13:4–5).

With calmness and majesty, in total silence, Jesus stood up, walked over and took the pitcher, and poured the water into the basin. He then removed his outer robe, His belt, and very likely His inner tunic—leaving Him clothed like a slave—put a towel around His waist, and knelt to wash the feet of His disciples, one by one.

Can you imagine how that must have stung the disciples' hearts? What pain, regret, and sorrow must have shot through them as they were about to learn a profound lesson. One of them could have had the joy of kneeling and washing the feet of Jesus. I'm sure they were dumbfounded and broken-hearted.

We, too, can learn from this incident. Sadly, the church is full of people who are standing on their dignity when they ought to be kneeling at the feet of their brothers and sisters. The desire for prominence is death to love, death to humility, and death to service. One who is proud and self-centered has no capacity for love or humility. Consequently, any service he may think he is performing for the Lord is a waste.

When you are tempted to think of your dignity, your prestige, or your rights, open your Bible to John 13 and get a good look at Jesus—clothed like a slave, kneeling, washing dirt off the feet of sinful men who are utterly indifferent to His impending death. To go from being God in glory (v. 3) to washing the feet of sinful, unglorious disciples (vv. 4–5) is a long step. Think about this: The majestic, glorious God of the universe comes to earth—that's humility. Then He kneels on the ground to wash the feet of sinful men—that's indescribable humility.

For a fisherman to wash the feet of another fisherman is a relatively small sacrifice of dignity. But that Jesus Christ, in whose heart beat the pulse of eternal deity, would stoop down and wash the feet of lowly men—that is the greatest kind of humiliation. And that is the nature of genuine humility, as well as the proof of genuine love.

Love has to be more than words. The Apostle John wrote, "Let us not love in word or in tongue, but in deed and in truth" (1 John 3:18). Love that is real is love expressed in activity, not just words.

"IF I DO NOT WASH YOU,
YOU HAVE NO PART WITH ME"

Next, John 13 gives us one of the most interesting insights into Peter's personality that we see anywhere in Scripture. As Jesus lovingly moved from disciple to disciple, He finally arrived at Peter. Peter must have been completely broken and he said with a mixture of remorse and incredulity, "'Lord, are You washing my feet?'" (v. 6), perhaps pulling them back.

Jesus replied to Peter, "'What I am doing you do not understand now, but you will know after this'" (v. 7). At this point, Peter was still thinking that the kingdom was coming, and Jesus was the King. How could he allow the King to wash his feet? It wasn't until after the Savior's death, resurrection, and ascension that Peter understood the total humiliation of Jesus.

Peter got bolder. "'You shall never wash my feet!'" (v. 8). To emphasize his words, Peter used the strongest form of negation in the Greek language. He called Jesus Lord, but he did not defer to His lordship. That was not praiseworthy modesty by Peter.

"Jesus answered him, 'If I do not wash you, you have no part with Me.' Simon Peter said to Him, 'Lord, not my feet only, but also my hands and my head!'" (vv. 8–9). That was typical of Peter—he went from one extreme ("You shall never wash my feet!") to the other ("Not my feet only, but also my hands and my head!")

There is profound meaning in Jesus' words, "If I do not wash you, you have no part with Me." The typical Jewish mindset could not accept the Messiah humiliated. In Peter's mind, therefore, there was no place for Christ to be humiliated as He was. So Jesus had to make him realize that the Christ came to be humiliated. If Peter could not accept this act of foot washing, he would certainly have trouble accepting what Jesus would do for him on the cross.

There is yet another, more profound, truth in Jesus' words. He has moved from the physical illustration of washing feet to the spiritual truth of washing the inner person. Throughout John's gospel, when He dealt with people, Jesus spoke of spiritual truth in physical terms. He did it when He spoke to Nicodemus, the woman at the well, and the Pharisees. Now He does it with Peter.

He is saying, "Peter, unless you allow Me to wash you in a spiritual way, you are not clean and you have no part with Me." All cleansing in the spiritual realm comes from Christ, and the only way anyone can be clean is if he is washed by regeneration through Jesus Christ (Titus 3:5). No one has a relationship with Jesus Christ unless Christ has cleansed his sins. And no one can enter into the presence of the Lord unless he first submits to that cleansing.

Peter learned that truth—he preached it himself in Acts 4:12: "Nor is there salvation in any other, for there is no other name under heaven given among men by which we must be saved." When a person puts his faith in Jesus Christ, he's clean, but not until then.

"HE WHO IS BATHED . . . IS COMPLETELY CLEAN"

Thinking that the Lord was speaking of physical cleansing, Peter offered his hands and head—everything. He still did not see the full spiritual meaning, but he said in essence, "Whatever washing you've got to offer me that makes me a part of You, I want it."

Jesus, still speaking of spiritual washing, said, " 'He who is bathed needs only to wash his feet, but is completely clean; and you are clean' " (John 13:10). There is a difference between a bath and a foot washing. In the culture of that day, a person would take a bath in the morning to get himself completely clean. As he went through the day, he periodically had to wash his feet, because of the dusty roads, but he didn't have to keep taking baths. All he needed was to wash the dirt off his feet when he entered someone's home.

Jesus is saying this: Once your inner person has been bathed in redemption, you are clean. From that point on, you do not need a new bath—you do not need to be redeemed again—every time you commit a sin. All God has to do is daily get the dust off your feet. Positionally, you are clean (as He told Peter in verse 10), but on the practical side, you need washing every day, as you walk through the world and get dirty feet.

That spiritual washing of the feet is what 1 John 1:9 refers to: "If we confess our sins, He is faithful and just to forgive us our sins and to cleanse us [literally, keep on cleansing us] from all unrighteousness."

Jesus knew which of the disciples was truly cleansed by redemption. Furthermore, He knew what Judas' plans for the evening were: "For He knew who would betray Him; therefore He said, 'You are not all clean'" (John 13:11). That should have convicted the heart of Judas.

Judas knew what He meant. Those words, combined with Jesus' washing his feet, constituted what would be the last loving appeal for Judas not to do what he was planning to do. What was going through the mind of Judas as Jesus knelt washing his feet? Whatever it was, it did not deter his evil plans.

"YOU ALSO OUGHT TO WASH ONE ANOTHER'S FEET"

Notice what happened after Jesus finished washing the disciples' feet:

> So when He had washed their feet, taken His garments, and sat down again, He said to them, "Do you know what I have done to you? You call Me Teacher and Lord, and you say well, for so I am. If I then, your Lord and Teacher, have washed your feet, you also ought to wash one another's feet. For I have given you an example, that you should do as I have done to you. Most assuredly, I say to you, a servant is not greater than his master; nor is he who is sent greater than he who sent him. If you know these things, blessed are you if you do them." (John 13:12–17)

Having inserted a parenthetical lesson on salvation—a sort of theological interlude—Jesus returned to the real point He was teaching His disciples: that they needed to begin to demonstrate humility.

He argued from the greater to the lesser. If the Lord of glory was willing to gird Himself with a towel, assume the form of a servant, act like a slave, and wash the dirty feet of sinful disciples, it was reasonable that the disciples should have been willing to wash each other's feet. The visual example Jesus taught surely did more good than a lecture on humility ever would have. It was something the disciples never forgot. (Perhaps from then on they had a contest to see who got to the water first!)

Many people believe that Jesus was instituting an ordinance for the church. Some churches practice foot washing in a ritual manner similar to the way most of us observe baptism and communion. I have no quarrel with that, but I do not believe this passage is teaching such a view. Jesus was not advocating a formal, ritualistic foot-washing service.

Verse 15 says, "'For I have given you an example, that you should do as I have done to you.'" The word "as" is a translation of the Greek word *kathos,* which means "according as." If He were establishing foot washing as an ordinance to be practiced in the church, He would have used the Greek word *ho,* which means "that which." Then He would have been saying, "I have given you an example that you should do what I have done to you."

He is not saying, "Do the same thing I have done." Rather He is saying, "Behave in the same manner as I have behaved." The example we are to follow is not the washing of feet, it is His humility. Do not minimize Jesus' lesson by trying to make foot washing the important point of John 13. His humility is the real lesson—and it is a practical humility that governs every area of life, every day of life, in every experience of life.

The result of that kind of humility is always loving service—doing the menial and humiliating tasks for the glory of Jesus Christ—which demolishes most of the popular ideas of what constitutes spirituality.

Some people seem to think that the nearer you get to God the further you must be from humanity, but that's not true. Genuine proximity to God is to serve someone else.

There was never any sacrificial service to others that Jesus was unwilling to perform. Why should we be different? We are not greater than the Lord: "'Most assuredly, I say to you, a servant is not greater than his master; nor is he who is sent greater than he who sent him. If you know these things, blessed are you if you do them'" (vv. 16–17).

Do you want to be blessedly fulfilled and happy? Develop a servant's heart. We are His bond-servants, and a servant is not greater than his master. If Jesus can step down from a position of deity to become a man, and then further humble Himself to be a servant and wash the feet of twelve undeserving sinners, we ought to be willing to suffer any indignity to serve Him. That is true love, and true humility.

TWO

UNMASKING THE BETRAYER

JUDAS ISCARIOT, WHO BETRAYED THE SON OF GOD WITH A KISS, has become the most despised person in the annals of human history. His personality is one of the darkest ever chronicled, and the name Judas itself bears a stigma, reflecting the scorn everyone feels for him. The New Testament writers disdain Judas to such a degree that in every list of the disciples given in the Gospels, Judas is listed last, with a note of contempt after his name.

Hatred for Judas Iscariot was so deep in the years following the closing of the New Testament canon that several incredible legends about him evolved. They describe bizarre occurrences, characterizing Judas as ugly, evil, and totally repugnant. One, in the apocryphal *Coptic Narrative,* said that Judas, having betrayed Christ, was infested with maggots. Consequently, his body became so large and bloated that on one occasion as he was trying to ride on a cart through a gate his oversized body hit the gate, exploded, and showered maggots all over the wall. Obviously, that story is not true, but it vividly illustrates the high level of contempt for Judas in the early centuries.

When I was in seminary, I wrote my dissertation on the subject of Judas. Since then, I have found it extremely difficult to write or teach about the man who betrayed Jesus. Sin is never more grotesque than it is in the life of Judas. When we study Judas and his motivations, we are prying very close to the activity of Satan. But there are valuable reasons for examining Judas and his sin. For one thing, to understand Jesus' love in its fullness, it helps to look at the life of Judas. There we learn that, despite the awfulness of Judas' sin, Jesus reached out to him in love.

JESUS AND JUDAS

In John 13:18–30, Jesus and Judas come head to head. We see clearly at this point the evil of Judas contrasted with the absolute purity of Jesus Christ. The diabolical deed that had been festering in the heart of Judas—the treachery he had already begun to perpetrate—was pushed to its climax, and Jesus unmasked Judas as the betrayer.

Jesus is speaking at the beginning of this powerful passage:

> "I do not speak concerning all of you. I know whom I have chosen; but that the Scripture may be fulfilled, 'He who eats bread with Me has lifted up his heel against Me.' Now I tell you before it comes, that when it does come to pass, you may believe that I am He. Most assuredly, I say to you, he who receives whomever I send receives Me; and he who receives Me receives Him who sent Me."
>
> When Jesus had said these things, He was troubled in spirit, and testified and said, "Most assuredly, I say to you, one of you will betray Me." Then the disciples looked at one another, perplexed about whom He spoke.
>
> Now there was leaning on Jesus' bosom one of His disciples, whom Jesus loved. Simon Peter therefore motioned to him to ask who it was of whom He spoke.
>
> Then, leaning back on Jesus' breast, he said to Him, "Lord, who is it?"
>
> Jesus answered, "It is he to whom I shall give a piece of bread when I have dipped it." And having dipped the bread, He gave it to

Judas Iscariot, the son of Simon. Now after the piece of bread, Satan entered him. Then Jesus said to him, "What you do, do quickly." But no one at the table knew for what reason He said this to him. For some thought, because Judas had the money box, that Jesus had said to him, "Buy those things we need for the feast," or that he should give something to the poor.

Having received the piece of bread, he then went out immediately. And it was night.

There we see Jesus and Judas as the epitome of opposites: the Perfect One and the absolutely wretched one; the best and the worst. The purity of Jesus and the vileness of Judas were displayed in sharp contrast.

The story of Judas is an ultimate tragedy—probably the greatest tragedy ever lived out. He is the prime example of what it means to have opportunity and then lose it. His story becomes all the more terrible because of the glorious beginnings he had. For three years, day in and day out, he occupied himself with Jesus Christ. He saw the same miracles, heard the same words, performed some of the same ministries, was esteemed in the same way the other disciples were esteemed—yet he did not become what the others became. In fact, he became the very opposite. While they were growing into true apostles and saints of God, he was progressively turning into a vile, calculating tool of Satan.

Initially, Judas must have shared the same hope of the kingdom that the other disciples had. He likely believed that Jesus was the Messiah. Certainly at some point he became greedy, but it is doubtful that he joined the apostles merely for what money he could get because they never really had anything. Perhaps his motive at the outset was just to get in on the benefits of the Messianic kingdom. Whatever his character at the beginning, Judas gradually became the treacherous man who betrayed Christ, a man who had no thought for anyone but himself, a man who finally wanted only to get as much money as he could and then get away.

By the end, greed, ambition, and worldliness had crept into Judas' heart, and avarice became his besetting sin. Perhaps he was also disappointed because of unfulfilled expectations of an earthly kingdom. Maybe he was tormented by the unbearable rebuke of the presence of Christ. Surely it created a great tension in his heart to be constantly in the presence of sinless purity, and yet be so infested with vileness. Perhaps, too, he began to sense that the eye of the Master could discern his true nature. All those things likely had begun to eat at him.

Whatever the reasons, Judas' life ended in absolute disaster, the greatest example of lost opportunity the world has ever seen. On the night he betrayed Jesus, he was so prepared to do Satan's bidding that the devil was able to enter him and take complete control. A few days before this, in Bethany, he had met with the leaders of Israel and bargained for thirty pieces of silver, the price of a slave—about twenty-five to thirty dollars. Now his evil deed came to full fruition on the eve of the crucifixion.

Jesus and His disciples (including Judas) were in the upper room. The vile traitor was sitting there, having already initiated his plot to betray Jesus and now spending these moments with the other disciples, looking for the best opportunity to betray Jesus' presence to the Jewish leaders.

Jesus had revealed that He knew Judas' heart, saying, " 'You are clean, but not all of you.' For He knew who would betray Him" (John 13:10–11). Judas had been sitting there all through Jesus' wonderful lesson on humility, taught by the washing of the disciples' feet. Jesus had even washed his feet. The wretched hypocrite had sat there, letting the blessed Lord wash his feet, while barely able to wait to get his hands on the thirty coins.

Even though Jesus knew what Judas was about to do, He still washed his feet. It was only one example of the marvelous love of Jesus Christ and the way He reached out to Judas. The measures He took to win Judas, even at this late hour, made His love all the more wonderful. One would think the experience of having Jesus wash his feet would have been enough to break any man's heart. But Judas' heart was so cold and hard that he remained determined to sell the Master to the executioners.

THE BLESSED AND THE CURSED

Having taught by example a wonderful lesson on humility, Jesus then carefully explained the lesson's meaning. He concluded His discourse by saying, "'If you know these things, blessed are you if you do them'" (John 13:17) "Blessed," of course, is a synonym for happy. One who learns how to show humble love, is willing to bow down to the ground and serve another believer, is the one rewarded with true happiness. When you condescend in that kind of love, when you're willing to do that menial duty for the sake of another, when you don't care about having the preeminence in every situation—when you humble yourself—you will be happy.

But Jesus could not speak of blessedness without speaking of the contrast. He did not think of happiness without thinking of tragedy and unhappiness. In that regard, His mind began to fill with thoughts of the cursed Judas sitting beside Him. Therefore, He turned His focus from the happy disciples to the cursed one, Judas (John 13:18). From verses 18 to 30 the dialogue centers on Judas himself. This is the final confrontation between Jesus and Judas, leaving only a kiss later on.

It is important to understand why Jesus brought up the subject of His betrayal at this point. Unless Jesus had in some way prepared the disciples for what was about to happen, the betrayal could have had a serious, adverse affect on them. If Judas had suddenly and without warning betrayed Jesus, the disciples may have concluded that Jesus wasn't all He claimed to be; otherwise He would have known that Judas was like this and never would have chosen him. So Jesus said, "'I know whom I have chosen; but that the Scripture may be fulfilled, "He who eats bread with Me has lifted up his heel against Me."'" Now

I tell you before it comes, that when it does come to pass, you may believe that I am He'" (v. 18). Jesus wanted to be sure they did not think He was surprised by what Judas was about to do. He therefore said in effect to those disciples, "I know I chose Judas. I did it, not by accident, not in ignorance, but that Scripture might be fulfilled." He chose Judas because Judas was necessary to bring about His death, which was necessary to bring about the redemption of His own.

As we are about to see, prophecy was clear that a close friend would betray Christ. Why did Jesus choose Judas, then? He chose him to fulfill prophecy—not only the prophecy specifically about Judas, but also the prophecies of His own death. Somebody had to bring these to pass, and Judas was more than willing. God used the wrath of Judas to praise Him, and through Judas' deed He brought salvation. Judas meant it for evil, but God used it for good (cf. Gen. 50:20).

GOD'S PLAN AND JUDAS' PLOT

Judas fit right into God's sovereign, master plan of redemption. Judas' betrayal was predicted in detail in the Old Testament. Psalm 41:9 says, "Even my own familiar friend in whom I trusted, who ate my bread, has lifted up his heel against me." That psalm has historical as well as prophetic meaning. It is David's lament over his own betrayal by his trusted adviser and friend Ahithophel. David had a wayward son named Absalom. Absalom decided to start a rebellion, overthrow his father, and take over the throne. Ahithophel turned against David and joined Absalom's rebellion. The picture of David and Ahithophel in Psalm 41 is fulfilled in a greater sense in Jesus and Judas. The phrase "lifted up his heel" portrays brutal violence—the lifting of a heel and the driving of it into the neck of the victim. That is the picture of Judas. Having already wounded his enemy, who is now lying on the ground, he takes the giant heel and crushes his neck.

18

Psalm 55 contains another clear prophecy of Judas and his betrayal. Imagine Jesus speaking these words:

> For it is not an enemy who reproaches me; then I could bear it. Nor is it one who hates me who has exalted himself against me; then I could hide from him. But it was you, a man my equal, my companion and my acquaintance. We took sweet counsel together, and walked to the house of God in the throng.

> He has put forth his hands against those who were at peace with him; he has broken his covenant. The words of his mouth were smoother than butter, but war was in his heart; his words were softer than oil, yet they were drawn swords. (vv. 12–14, 20–21)

Zechariah contains a prophecy about the betrayal of Christ by Judas in even more detail. It gives the exact price he was paid for his treachery, just as it is recorded in the New Testament. Zechariah 11:12–13 prophesies the words of Judas, talking to the Jewish leaders: "Then I said to them, 'If it is agreeable to you, give me my wages; and if not, refrain.' So they weighed out for my wages thirty pieces of silver. And the LORD said to me, 'Throw it to the potter'—that princely price they set on me. So I took the thirty pieces of silver and threw them into the house of the LORD for the potter."

That describes to the letter what Judas did after the death of Jesus Christ. He took the thirty pieces right back to the house of the Lord and threw them down. Matthew 27, exactly fulfilling the prophecy of Zechariah 11, says the thirty pieces were picked up and used to buy a potter's field.

Jesus' choosing Judas was no accident. Long before Judas was ever born, his hatred of Christ was planned by divine design—predestined in the plan of God from eternity past. In John 17:12 Jesus, praying to the Father, says of the disciples, "While I was with them in the world, I kept them in Your name. Those whom You gave Me I have kept; and none of them is lost except the son of perdition, that the Scripture might be fulfilled."

DIVINE SOVEREIGNTY AND HUMAN CHOICE

Judas' role was not apart from his own will. Even though God ordained him as the disciple who would betray Christ, it was not apart from the desire of Judas. Judas was no robot. Our Lord did not simply allocate to an unwilling Judas the part of the villain in the crucifixion. Such a thing would be inconsistent with the character of Jesus Christ. It is also inconsistent with the historical record. During Jesus' ministry, He endeavored to drive Judas to repentance, time and time again, with His love, His pleas, and His rebukes. So although Judas' treachery fit into the plan of God, God did not design him as a treacherous man. He became a traitor to Christ by his own choice. God merely took Judas, wretched and treacherous as he was, and fitted him into His plan. If God were responsible for making Judas what he was, Jesus would have pitied him rather than rebuked him. Judas Iscariot, then, in accordance with his own will, was the chosen instrument of God to betray Christ and help bring about His death.

WALKING WITH JESUS BUT FOLLOWING SATAN

Judas, through his life of treachery, supplies sinners with a solemn warning. We learn from the example of Judas that a person can be very near to Jesus Christ and yet be lost and damned forever. Nobody was ever closer to Christ than the Twelve. Judas was one of them, but he is nevertheless in hell today. While he may have given intellectual assent to the truth, he never embraced Christ with heartfelt faith.

Judas wasn't deceived; he was a phony. He understood the truth, and he posed as a believer. Furthermore, he was good at what he did—the cleverest hypocrite we read about in all the Scriptures, for no one ever suspected him. He had everyone fooled except Jesus, who knew his heart.

Wherever God's work is done, there are impostors like Judas. There will always be hypocrites among the brethren. The favorite trick of Satan and those he employs is to "transform themselves into ministers of righteousness" (2 Cor. 11:15). The devil is a master at making his work look good—and he is busily at work among the Lord's people.

TRUTH AND CONSEQUENCES

Prior to the last Passover meal with His disciples, Jesus had maintained secrecy about Judas' hypocrisy. Now He determined to reveal the truth, knowing that if the other eleven disciples were taken by surprise, their faith might have been undermined. As we noted above, He wanted them to know that He was not being taken by surprise, that God is never any man's victim. He wanted to ensure that when He was gone, their faith would be strong.

In revealing to them the truth about Judas, He also irrefutably affirmed His deity. In John 13:19, He says, "'Now I tell you before it comes, that when it does come to pass, you may believe that I am He.'" (The "He" in that verse is not in the original Greek text.) "I am" is God's name (cf. Exod. 3:14) Jesus is in essence saying, "I want you to know that I am God, and I knew this would happen." Thus He affirmed His name and established His omniscience. Nothing is hidden from His sight. He knows what goes on in Christians' hearts, but more than that, He knows what goes on in the hearts of unregenerate people as well. In John 5:42 Jesus, talking to unbelieving Jews, says, "'But I know you, that you do not have the love of God in you.'" He knows the heart of every person, believer or unbeliever, and reads them like open books.

21

THE APOSTLES AND THE BETRAYER

In John 13:20, after affirming His deity and still speaking of His imminent betrayal, Jesus says, "'Most assuredly, I say to you, he who receives whomever I send receives Me; and he who receives Me receives Him who sent Me.'" Initially, that statement doesn't seem to fit the context of what Jesus was teaching. But a closer look reveals that it fits beautifully.

We don't know what occurred during the gap between verses 19 and 20. But you can imagine that, when the disciples found out about the betrayal, they might all have assumed that because of the failure of one of them credibility would be destroyed for the rest. They might have assumed that a traitor among the disciples would lower the standing of them all. If Jesus went to the Cross, they must have thought, the Messianic hope would be gone. Their ministry would be over. They might as well forget about the kingdom. And since Jesus had just been stressing the importance of humility, the disciples might have thought He was telling them to forget about their high calling.

What Jesus was actually saying is this: "No matter what happens, it doesn't lower your commission, and it doesn't alter your calling. You are still my representatives. Although there's a traitor among you, that doesn't affect your high calling. The treachery of Judas must never lower your estimate of apostolic responsibility." It was a tremendous lesson for them. He's saying, "When you go out there and preach, if they receive you they are receiving Me. And if they receive Me, they are receiving the Father who sent Me. Your commission is that high. You represent God in the world."

When Christ was crucified, Judas turned out to be a despicable hypocrite, and the whole world seemed to be collapsing, it was easy for the disciples to hit bottom spiritually and emotionally. So Jesus took the opportunity to elevate them and encourage them to keep their focus where it belonged—on their calling and ministry.

We need to be aware of that truth as well. No matter what Satanic opposition we run into, no matter how frustrating our ministry becomes, nothing can lower our commission. I once talked to a discouraged man in the Lord's service. He was facing so much opposition that he was beginning to wonder if he was in the right place. But I told him opposition is to be expected. Anything we do for God is going to meet with opposition. If every missionary looked at a mission field and said, "Oh, they might not believe me over there," the church would never get anything done. Just because it's going to be difficult, and just because there's going to be opposition, that doesn't lower our calling. We are Christ's ambassadors in the world. Those who reject us reject Christ. So regardless of what happens, we ought to stand with Him. That's the highest calling.

When a believer moves out into this world, he represents Jesus Christ. Paul says in 2 Corinthians 5:20, "Now then, we are ambassadors for Christ, as though God were pleading through us: we implore you on Christ's behalf, be reconciled to God." In Galatians 4:14, the Apostle Paul says, "You received me as an angel of God, even as Christ Jesus." And that's the way everybody ought to receive a believer. When a person rejects our witness for Christ, he rejects Jesus the Son and God the Father. That's how strategically important believers are. And that's Jesus' point in John 13:20. Notice that He uses the word "whomever." That refers to His ambassadors in every age, including those of us who represent Him today.

Have you ever heard someone use the existence of hypocrites in the church as an excuse for not following Christ? People often say, "There are too many hypocrites in the church for me." Or, "Well, we don't go to church, because we went when I was nine and we saw a hypocrite. Haven't been back in forty-two years!" That will be a pathetic excuse when they present it to God at the judgment seat.

It is true that there are too many hypocrites in the church. They're everywhere. And one hypocrite is one too many. But the fact that some are hypocrites does not diminish the glory of God or lower the high calling of every true child of God. One betrayer among the apostles did not tarnish the commission of the rest.

WHEAT AND TARES

In Matthew 13:24–30, Jesus gives this parable:

"The kingdom of heaven is like a man who sowed good seed in his field; but while men slept, his enemy came and sowed tares among the wheat and went his way. But when the grain had sprouted and produced a crop, then the tares also appeared. So the servants of the owner came and said to him, 'Sir, did you not sow good seed in your field? How then does it have tares?' He said to them, 'An enemy has done this.' The servants said to him, 'Do you want us then to go and gather them up?' But he said, 'No, lest while you gather up the tares you also uproot the wheat with them. Let both grow together until the harvest, and at the time of harvest I will say to the reapers, "First gather together the tares and bind them in bundles to burn them, but gather the wheat into my barn."'"

In other words, it was hard to tell the difference between wheat and tares before everything was ready for harvest. And although there may be some telltale signs, we can't always tell the difference between the true people of God and the hypocrites. If we knew which was which, we could go to every hypocrite individually and warn him of the danger of his hypocrisy. But we can't read people's hearts. Some day Jesus is going to reveal who is true and who is false, and He will divide accordingly.

THE TROUBLED HEART AND THE HARDENED HEART

Unmasking Judas' betrayal must have caused deep anguish within the heart of Jesus. "When Jesus had said these things, He was troubled in spirit, and testified and said, 'Most assuredly, I say to you, one of you will betray Me'" (John 13:21). What troubled Him? Possibly a number of realities and several reasons: His unrequited love for Judas; the ingratitude in Judas' heart; He had a deep hatred of sin, and sitting at the same table with Him was sin incarnate; the hypocrisy of the one about to betray Him; He knew Judas faced an eternal residence in hell; He could see with His omnipotent eye Satan surrounding Judas; He perfectly sensed all that sin and death meant. But perhaps most of all Jesus was troubled because He had an awareness that Judas was a classic illustration of the kind of wretchedness sin produces, the entirety of which He would have to bear personally on the cross the next day.

In His anguish Christ said, "One of you will betray Me." Imagine the shock that must have struck the disciples. Their hearts must have raced when they realized it was one of those at the table, one whose feet Jesus had just washed; one of their own close-knit group was about to betray the Master. One of them was plotting to use his intimacy with Christ to help the enemy find Him and kill Him. It must have been difficult for them to fathom that one of their own could have such hardened treachery in his heart.

In fact, the disciples couldn't imagine whom He could be talking about. John says they "looked at one another, perplexed about whom He spoke" (13:22). Matthew says they all said, "Lord, is it I?" And Judas, the hypocrite, even said, "Rabbi, is it I?" (Matt. 26:22, 25).

LOVE AND TREACHERY

It is noteworthy that the disciples were so perplexed. It shows that Jesus had shown love to Judas for three years, even though He knew Judas would betray Him in the end. If Jesus had ever treated Judas any differently from the way He treated the other disciples—if He had been more distant, or shown resentment—they would have known immediately that Judas was the betrayer. If Jesus had harbored any bitterness for what He knew Judas would ultimately do, it would have come out in the way He talked to him. But, evidently, for three years He had been gentle, loving, and kind to Judas, treating Him in exactly the same manner He treated the other eleven. They thought of him as one of the group, and no one suspected him of treachery.

In fact, they must have had a great deal of trust in him since Judas was their treasurer. But hard-hearted Judas had just played his game. He had the behavior of a saint but the heart of a sinner. He must have come to hate Christ deeply.

The hatred of Judas and the love of John make an interesting contrast. Try to picture the scene around the table. The table itself would have been U-shaped. In accordance with the customs of that time, the disciples would not have been seated on chairs, but rather reclining on couches. The table would have been a low, solid block with the couches around it and the host (Jesus) seated at the center. On each side of Him would have been His closest disciples (guests of honor), and others would have been positioned all around the table. They would have lain on their left sides, resting on their left elbows, using their right hands to eat. Thus the one who was on the right of Jesus would have had his head very close to the heart of Christ. From a distance, it would have appeared that he was reclining on the Lord's breast.

John, who wrote this account, often referred to himself as "the disciple whom Jesus loved" (John 21:20; cf. 21:24). It was not that Jesus loved him more than He loved the others, but rather that John was completely overwhelmed with the concept that Jesus loved him at all. Also, John was consumed with love for the Lord. He loved Jesus as much as Judas hated Him.

John writes: "Now there was leaning on Jesus' bosom one of His disciples, whom Jesus loved. Simon Peter therefore motioned to him to ask who it was of whom He spoke" (John 13:23–24). Peter silently motioned to John to ask Jesus who the betrayer would be. So John leaned up and whispered, "Lord, who is it?" When he turned to speak with Him, Christ was very close.

"Jesus answered, 'It is he to whom I shall give a piece of bread when I have dipped it.' And having dipped the bread, He gave it to Judas Iscariot, the son of Simon" (v. 26). Jesus' answer to Peter and John was really a final appeal of love to Judas. The "piece of bread" was a piece broken from some of the unleavened cakes that were on the table as a part of the Passover feast. Also on the table was a dish called cheshireth, filled with bitter herbs, vinegar, salt, and mashed fruit (consisting of dates, figs, raisins, and water)—all mixed together into a pasty substance. Jesus and His disciples ate it with the unleavened bread like a dip.

It was a mark of honor for the host to dip a morsel into the cheshireth and give it to the guest of honor. And Jesus, in a kind gesture of love toward Judas, dipped the morsel and gave it to him, as if Judas were the guest of honor. One would think that all Jesus had done for Judas that night would have broken his heart, but it didn't. Judas was an apostate. His heart was hardened, and nothing Jesus could do for him would break it. Salvation for him was now impossible. He had become the classic example of the kind of person the writer of Hebrews describes: "For it is impossible for those who were once enlightened, and have tasted the heavenly gift, and have become partakers of the Holy Spirit, and have tasted the good word of God and the powers of the age to come, if they fall away, to renew them again to repentance, since they crucify again for themselves the Son of God, and put Him to an open shame" (Heb. 6:4–6). He had seen and experienced and tasted all those things, but he had never embraced them with true faith.

Judas was so confirmed in his apostasy that Satan literally possessed him. John 13:27 says, "Now after the piece of bread, Satan entered him. Then Jesus said to him, 'What you do, do quickly.'" Satan had duped Judas, following the long period Judas had been flirting with him. Satan had already put it into his heart to betray Christ, and now, Satan simply moved in and took over. In that awful moment, the evil will of Judas rejected the last and most powerful offer of Jesus Christ's love, and the sin against the Holy Spirit was finalized. In that moment, Judas was damned to hell forever. He had spurned the love of Christ for the last time and his eternity was sealed.

DAY AND NIGHT

Jesus' attitude toward Judas immediately changed. He was through with Judas. The betrayer had crossed the line of grace, and no more could Jesus reach out to him. The difference was immediate, radical—like day and night. Jesus had been reaching out to Judas in love, but Judas was confirmed in his stubborn apostasy. All Jesus wanted now was to get rid of him.

Notice that Satan and Jesus were now giving Judas the same direction. Satan said, "Betray Him." Christ said, "Do it quickly." Judas was clearly determined to betray Christ, Satan was determined to destroy Him, and Christ was determined to die for a multitude of sinners. (Jesus would in the end shatter Satan's plan by emerging triumphant from the grave.)

None of the disciples caught the significance of what was occurring. "But no one at the table knew for what reason He said this to him. For some thought, because Judas had the money box, that Jesus had said to him, 'Buy those things we need for the feast,' or that he should give something to the poor" (John 13:28–29). They thought he was going shopping, or out to dispense some charity at the Passover season.

"Having received the piece of bread, he then went out immediately. And it was night" (v. 30). There he went, a solitary figure leaving the room to enter into the eternal grip of hell. The Bible doesn't say where he went, but evidently he went to finalize his deal with the Sanhedrin. And when he went out, it was night. For Judas, who had walked with Jesus and yet stayed in darkness, the hours of daylight and opportunity were over. It was more than mere physical night, it was eternal night in the soul of Judas. It is always night when someone flees from the presence of Jesus Christ.

There are Judases in every age. Perhaps they are more common than ever today. The professing church is full of people who sell out Jesus Christ and "crucify again for themselves the Son of God, and put Him to an open shame" (Heb. 6:6). There are many who have eaten at His table, and then lifted their heel against Him. And the greatest tragedy still is only their own ultimate disaster. A poem I once read includes these few poignant words:

> Still as of old,
> By himself is priced.
> For thirty pieces Judas sold
> Himself, not Christ.

Be sure that you make the most of your opportunities. Be sure you're not a hypocrite. If we learn anything from the life of Judas, it is that the greatest spiritual privileges can be neutralized by unrepentant sinful desires and a commitment to evil priorities. A life that is lived in the face of the unclouded Sun may yet end in a night of despair.

THREE

THE MARKS OF THE COMMITTED CHRISTIAN

Historically, Christians have displayed a number of different kinds of symbols to mark their identity as believers. They have used such emblems as lapel pins and neck chains with gold crosses, almost since the beginning of Christianity, to identify themselves as followers of Christ. In recent years, people have also used such items as bumper stickers, posters, tee shirts, decorated Bibles, and jackets with embroidered insignia. I don't have any argument with such symbols, except that they are totally superficial—only as deep as the surface to which they are attached.

As a Christian, whether or not you wear a button, display a bumper sticker, or use any other kind of visible symbol is of no real consequence. More important, and infinitely more definitive than all the pins and stickers and buttons, are the internal, spiritual signs of a true believer.

In John 13:31–38, Jesus gives three distinguishing marks of a committed Christian. As His earthly ministry was coming to an end, He was with His disciples the night before His death to prepare them for His leaving. With Judas banished from the ranks of the apostles, Jesus turned to the eleven remaining disciples and gave them a valedictory address.

So when he [Judas Iscariot] had gone out, Jesus said, "Now the Son of Man is glorified, and God is glorified in Him. If God is glorified in Him, God will also glorify Him in Himself, and glorify Him immediately. Little children, I shall be with you a little while longer. You will seek Me; and as I said to the Jews, 'Where I am going, you cannot come,' so now I say to you. A new commandment I give to you, that you love one another; as I have loved you, that you also love one another. By this all will know that you are My disciples, if you have love for one another."

Simon Peter said to Him, "Lord, where are You going?"

Jesus answered him, "Where I am going you cannot follow Me now, but you shall follow Me afterward."

Peter said to Him, "Lord, why can I not follow You now? I will lay down my life for Your sake."

Jesus answered him, "Will you lay down your life for My sake? Most assuredly, I say to you, the rooster shall not crow till you have denied Me three times."

This passage introduces Jesus' last commission to His disciples before He went to the cross. His farewell message, which continues through John 16, contains every ingredient we need to know about discipleship. In fact, the basics of Paul's teaching on the subject seem to match this portion of John. Thus these concluding words of our Lord on His last evening with His disciples are indispensable to knowing what Christ expects of us as believers. The three major characteristics of discipleship Jesus presents should be evident in the life of every believer.

AN UNENDING PREOCCUPATION
WITH THE GLORY OF GOD

First, the committed Christian is preoccupied and absorbed with his Lord's glory. The very purpose for which we exist is to give glory to God, so it is right that this is the first mark of a committed Christian.

He's not preoccupied with his own glory. He's not worried about what brings honor to him. He's not on a popularity binge. He's not trying to climb the ladder, to get something bigger and better for himself. He realizes that it doesn't matter how impressed people are with him, but only that they glorify God. His life reflects the attributes of God, and God is praised by the way he lives.

Jesus taught His disciples that perspective both by example and by precept: "So when he [Judas Iscariot] had gone out, Jesus said, 'Now the Son of Man is glorified, and God is glorified in Him. If God is glorified in Him, God will also glorify Him in Himself, and glorify Him immediately. Little children, I shall be with you a little while longer. You will seek Me; and as I said to the Jews, "Where I am going, you cannot come," so now I say to you'" (John 13:31–33).

The first phrase indicates almost a sense of relief from our Lord. Now that Judas was gone, He could speak freely to His disciples. God incarnate, Jesus Christ, had come to earth in humility. He had restricted the full manifestation of His glory and subjected Himself to human frailty, though He never sinned. For thirty-three years His glory had been shrouded in human flesh. By tomorrow He would be in His glory again. All the attributes of God would be on display in Him.

With His returning glory in mind, Jesus made three distinct statements. Each is unique and important for us to understand.

"Now the Son of Man is glorified"

The first is in verse 31, a great statement of anticipation: "'Now the Son of Man is glorified.'" Judas had already begun to set everything in motion. The Jews had already paid him for the betrayal, and he was now outside, getting everything set. In just a few hours, Jesus and the disciples would go into the Garden of Gethsemane, where Christ would continue His teaching. There Judas would march in with the soldiers and set in motion the events that would lead to Jesus' death.

Jesus was ready to die because, even though the cross looked like shame, disgrace, and disaster, it signified glory. At first it may seem difficult to understand how death can be glory, especially death by crucifixion. In His death our Lord experienced the deepest kind of shame, humiliation, accusation, insults, infamy, mockery, spitting, and all the abuse that men could throw at Him. He died hanging between thieves, receiving the agony of sin and separation from God. Yet knowing He was facing all of that, Jesus could say, "Now the Son of Man is glorified."

But was there really glory in the Cross? Yes, because on it Jesus performed the greatest work in the history of the universe. In His death He redeemed lost sinners, destroyed sin, and defeated Satan. He paid the price of God's justice and purchased for Himself all the elect of God. In dying for sin, He rendered His life a sweet-smelling savor to God, a sacrifice more pure and blessed than any ever offered. And when the sacrifice was completed, Jesus declared, "It is finished." He had accomplished the redemption of all those He came to seek and to save, satisfied the justice of God, repaired the broken law, and set free all who by faith embrace His glorious work. In all heaven and earth, no act is so worthy of praise, honor, and full glory. (For a thorough treatment of the significance and drama of Christ's death, see John MacArthur, *The Murder of Jesus* [Nashville: Word, 2000].)

"And God is glorified in Him"

Jesus made a second statement about glory. Not only was He glorified, but God was glorified in Him. God is glorified through the details of the gospel. When Jesus said, "'Now the Son of Man is glorified, and God is glorified in Him'" (v. 31), He was speaking of His death, burial, resurrection, exaltation, and coming again. All those events perfectly encompass the glory of God's redemptive plan.

One of the greatest ways we can glorify God is to declare the gospel. The message of the gospel radiates the glory of God like nothing else in all the universe. In a sense, therefore, witnessing is one of the highest and purest forms of worship.

God's glory is wrapped up in His attributes. His love, mercy, grace, wisdom, omniscience, omnipotence, omnipresence—all the attributes of God—reflect and declare His glory. We worship and glorify God when we in any way praise, acknowledge, experience, or display His attributes. When we are examples of His love, for instance, we glorify Him. When we acknowledge and yield to His sovereignty, we glorify Him.

At the Cross, every attribute of God was manifest in a way not seen before. The power of God, for example, was made visible on the cross. The kings and rulers of the earth took counsel together against God and against His Christ. The terrible enmity of the carnal mind and the desperate wickedness of the human heart nailed Jesus to a cross. The fiendish hatred of Satan put forth its best effort. The world, Satan, and every demon in the universe threw all the power they had at Christ, yet He had more than enough power to overcome it all. In death He broke every shackle, every dominance of sin, and every power of Satan forever. His graphic display of God's power thus glorified God.

The Cross revealed the justice of God in all its fullness. The wages of sin is death, and if God was going to redeem sinners, someone had to die for their sin. The penalty of the law had to be enforced, or God's justice would be compromised. Isaiah says that as Jesus hung there on the cross, "the LORD . . . laid on Him the iniquity of us all" (Isa. 53:6). God would not neglect justice, even if it meant the slaying of His beloved Son. Thus by paying the greatest price, Christ glorified God on the Cross by displaying His justice in the greatest possible way— more so than if every member of the human race were to suffer in hell forever.

God's holiness was also manifest at the Cross. Habakkuk wrote that God is "of purer eyes than to behold evil, and cannot look on wickedness" (Hab. 1:13). Never did God so manifest His hatred for sin as in the suffering and death of His own Son. As Christ suffered on the Cross, bearing the sins of the world, God turned away from His only begotten Son. Even though He loved Jesus Christ with an infinite love, His holiness could not tolerate looking at the Sin Bearer. That's why Jesus cried out in agony, "'My God, My God, why have You forsaken Me?'" (Matt. 27:46). All the cheerful obedience of godly people from every era is nothing compared to the offering of Christ Himself to satisfy every demand of God's holiness. Through that offering, God was glorified.

God's faithfulness also was displayed at the Cross. He had promised the world a Savior from the beginning. When Christ, the Sinless One, was offered on the Cross to receive the full and final wages of sin, God showed to all heaven and earth that He was faithful. Even though it cost Him His only Son, He went through with it. When we see that kind of faithfulness, we are seeing His glory.

Many other attributes of God were displayed in their fullness at the Cross, but the one that stands above all the others is the attribute of love. "In this is love, not that we loved God, but that He loved us and sent His Son to be the propitiation for our sins" (1 John 4:10). The human mind cannot comprehend the love that would cause God to have His Son die as an atonement for our sins. But He is glorified in the display of such love.

"God will also glorify Him"

In His third and final statement about glory, Jesus emphasizes the truth that the Father and the Son are busily engaged in glorifying each other, and the greatest glory of the Son is subsequent to His work on the cross. " 'If God is glorified in Him, God will also glorify Him in Himself, and glorify Him immediately' " (John 13:32). There was a certain glory in the Cross, but the Father would not stop there. The resurrection, the ascension, the exaltation of Christ in total glory are all important aspects of the glory that would be His. Even today, His greatest glory is yet future.

All that future glory for Christ meant that He had to leave. So He said, " 'Little children, I shall be with you a little while longer. You will seek Me; and as I said to the Jews, " 'Where I am going, you cannot come,' so now I say to you' " (v. 33). While His thoughts were on His glory and all the grandeur of it, He was also thinking about His eleven beloved disciples. He called them "little children"—an expression He probably would not have used if Judas had still been present.

What did He mean, "As I said to the Jews"? He told the Jews who sought to arrest Him, " 'You will seek Me and not find Me, and where I am you cannot come' " (John 7:34). John 8:21 says, "Then Jesus said to them again, 'I am going away, and you will seek Me, and will die in your sin. Where I go you cannot come.' " In verse 24 He adds, " 'Therefore I said to you that you will die in your sins; for if you do not believe that I am He, you will die in your sins.' "

It is significant that Jesus gave no such warning to His believing disciples. Although when He ascended they would not be able to follow Him where He was going, there was no danger they would die in their sins. Jesus was going to the Father, and they would miss His physical nearness, especially in times of trial and problems. In fact, in Acts 1, as Jesus ascended into heaven, they just stood there, gazing longingly into heaven. They didn't want Him to leave, and Jesus knew that. So in John 13, He is reassuring them that although His glory would involve His leaving, He still cared for them. It is the introduction of a theme that will carry through for the next few chapters of John.

Why did Jesus tell the disciples all this? Because He knew that as true disciples, their concern was for His glory. He wanted them to share the anticipation and the excitement of His coming glory. He wanted them to be preoccupied with thoughts of His glory.

A concern for God's glory, then, is one of the marks of a true disciple. It is the heart of the reason for our existence, a burning passion we inherit from our Lord Himself.

When Henry Martyn sailed for India, he said, "Let me burn out for God." Later, as he watched in a Hindu temple in India, he saw people prostrating themselves before images. He wrote in his diary, "This excited more horror in me than I can express." He continued, "I could not endure existence if Jesus was not glorified, it would be hell to me." Once somebody asked Martyn, "Why are you so preoccupied with His glory?" And he answered, "If someone plucks out your eyes, there's no saying why you feel pain, it is feeling—it is you. It is because I am one with Christ that I am so deeply wounded." Every genuine disciple knows something of that feeling.

AN UNFAILING LOVE FOR THE CHILDREN OF GOD

Not only is the committed disciple preoccupied with his Lord's glory, but he also is filled with His love. Perhaps this mark of the committed Christian is the most significant of all in terms of practical living that distinguishes us in the world.

Even though the apostles would no longer be able to rejoice in the visible presence of Jesus, they still would enjoy a full, rich experience of love, for they would have a depository of love in their own lives. In fact, love would be their primary distinguishing mark: "'A new commandment I give to you, that you love one another; as I have loved you, that you also love one another. By this all will know that you are My disciples, if you have love for one another'" (John 13:34–35). Those words of Christ had such a profound impact on the Apostle John that he made them his life's message: "'For this is the message that you heard from the beginning, that we should love one another'" (1 John 3:11).

As believers in Christ, we have a new God-given capacity to love. The love of Christ is poured out in our hearts (Rom. 5:5), and that love eliminates the necessity of a legal system (13:8–10). Because of love, we simply do not need to live by a set of rules and regulations. We don't need signs in our house that say, "Don't pistol-whip your wife"; "Don't bash your children with a hammer"; or "Don't steal, kill, or bear false witness." Genuine love makes all such rules superfluous.

What kind of love marks a true disciple? Jesus says, "Love one another as I have loved you." That sets the standard extremely high. Jesus' love is selfless, sacrificial, indiscriminate, understanding, and forgiving. Unless your love is like that, you have not fulfilled the new commandment.

If the church existed in that kind of love, we would absolutely overwhelm the world. Unfortunately, that isn't the way the professing church operates. There are factions, splits, and cliques. People gossip, backbite, talk too much, and criticize. People in the world look, and they don't see much love. So there is no way for them to know whether those who call themselves Christians are real or not.

One reason pseudo-Christian cults and false doctrines have so much influence today is that not many Christians are definitive disciples. It is often virtually impossible to distinguish a true disciple from a false one, for there isn't a lot of visible manifestation of God's love. Thus the world doesn't know who really possesses the truth. When the average person looks at the spectrum of "Christianity" and all that goes with it, he is baffled. Those around him who claim to be Christians seem to have no identifying marks, and if anything, they often seem to be more lacking in love than in any other character quality.

Earlier in John 13, as we've already discussed in chapter 1 of our study, Jesus taught the disciples by washing their feet that the key to love is humility. Here is how closely love is tied to humility: If you don't love, it's because you're proud. And God hates a proud heart. Those who are proud have no capacity for love. In Philippians 2:3–4, Paul says, "Let nothing be done through selfish ambition or conceit, but in lowliness of mind let each esteem others better than himself. Let each of you look out not only for his own interests, but also for the interests of others." That is exactly what Jesus did, and how He taught His disciples to love.

How can we manifest visible love? First, we can admit it when we have wronged someone. If you are not willing to go to somebody you have wronged and make things right, you call into question your commitment to Christ, and the church will suffer because of your unwillingness to love.

Most of the bitterness within the visible church has nothing to do with doctrinal differences. It derives instead from a fundamental lack of love, and an unwillingness to accept the humility that love demands. A second way to show love is by forgiving those who have wronged us—whether we are asked or not. No matter how serious the wrong you have suffered may be, love demands that you forgive it. Christ forgave those who had mocked Him, spit on Him, and then crucified Him. The wrongs we generally suffer seem insignificant compared to what He suffered, and yet how willing are we to follow His example and forgive immediately?

Scripture is clear and unyielding on this principle of unconditional forgiveness. First Corinthians 6:1 says, "Dare any of you, having a matter against another, go to law before the unrighteous?" (Some of the Corinthians were apparently suing other believers for wrongs that had been committed against them.) Verse 7 says, "Now therefore, it is already an utter failure for you that you go to law against one another. Why do you not rather accept wrong? Why do you not rather let yourselves be cheated?" No verse in all of Scripture is more practical and demanding than that.

Do you really want to maintain a testimony of love in this world? Then accept whatever comes your way, praise the Lord, and let His love flow through you to the one who wronged you. That kind of love would confound this world.

Real love is costly, and the one who truly loves will have to sacrifice, but while you sacrifice in this world you're gaining immeasurably in the spiritual realm. And you are displaying the most visible, practical, obvious mark of a true disciple.

AN UNSWERVING LOYALTY TO THE SON OF GOD

A third mark of the committed Christian is loyalty. It is more implied than expressed in the context of John 13. Nevertheless, loyalty is included with a marvellous illustration of Peter, who faltered often but ultimately proved himself to be a true disciple. From him we learn a number of intensely practical principles.

Discipleship is more than a promised loyalty. It must go beyond making a vow to God (which we tend to do glibly and frequently). Discipleship demands a practiced loyalty—an operating, functioning kind of loyalty that holds up under every kind of pressure.

All this talk about Jesus' going away must have deeply bothered Peter. He couldn't stand the thought of Jesus' leaving. Matthew 16:22 vividly shows how intensely Peter hated the thought of Jesus' impending death. Jesus had foretold His crucifixion and resurrection, and Peter, always the self-appointed spokesman for the disciples, took Jesus aside and began to rebuke Him: "'Far be it from You, Lord; this shall not happen to You!'" This was a stubborn, selfish attitude from Peter, who did not want Jesus to be taken from him under any conditions. Jesus "turned and said to Peter, 'Get behind Me, Satan! You are an offense to Me, for you are not mindful of the things of God, but the things of men'" (v. 23).

Jesus was completely aware of Peter's attitude, and He took the opportunity to teach Peter a lesson about true loyalty: "Simon Peter said to Him, 'Lord, where are You going?' Jesus answered him, 'Where I am going you cannot follow Me now, but you shall follow Me afterward.' Peter said to Him, 'Lord, why can I not follow you now? I will lay down my life for your sake.' Jesus answered him, 'Will you lay down your life for My sake? Most assuredly, I say to you, the rooster shall not crow till you have denied Me three times'" (John 13:36–38).

Peter's heart was burning with love for Jesus. But while his love for Jesus was admirable, his boasting was foolish. His refusal to accept Jesus' words was merely stubborn pride. In essence, he was saying, "If all You're going to do is die, I will be happy to die with You." But he was speaking rashly, as a braggart. Perhaps he said it for the benefit of the other disciples, but he was saying it in the flesh. Worst of all, the message to Jesus was, "I know better than You."

You can imagine what a shock it was to Peter when Jesus predicted that he would deny Him that very night. In fact, through the rest of the dialogue, Peter—uncharacteristically—never said another word.

Nevertheless, Matthew 26 reports that he repeated his boast again later that evening in the garden. That time all the disciples joined with him in affirming their absolute loyalty to Jesus, even if it meant dying (v. 35). But just a short time later, when their lives seemed truly to be on the line, "All the disciples forsook Him and fled" (v. 56).

There was a huge gap between their promised loyalty and their practiced loyalty. Peter, who had so loudly boasted that he would stand by the Lord, failed miserably. Instead of giving his life for Jesus, he tried to save it by denying Him. And he didn't do it in silence or by implication, he did it loudly with cursing, and before many witnesses. Four things made Peter fail the test of loyalty.

He boasted too much

First, Peter was too proud to listen to what Jesus was trying to tell him, and too busy boasting. Luke 22:31–32 records Jesus' admonition to Peter: "Simon, Simon! Indeed, Satan has asked for you, that he may sift you as wheat. But I have prayed for you, that your faith should not fail; and when you have returned to Me, strengthen your brethren." Implied in that warning is the prophecy that Peter would fail, and that he would later repent of his failure.

But Peter missed the whole point. "Lord, I am ready to go with You, both to prison and to death" (v. 33). First Kings 20:11 warns: "Let not the one who puts on his armor boast like the one who takes it off." Peter was boasting in his flesh, but he wasn't in a position to boast about anything.

He prayed too little

Peter also failed because his praying was not what it should have been. First, he was boasting while he should have been listening; and later that evening, he slept when he should have been praying. Sleep is a good thing, but it's not a substitute for prayer. While Jesus was praying in agony in Gethsemane, Peter and the other disciples fell asleep. Luke 22:45–46 says this: "When He rose up from prayer, and had come to His disciples, He found them sleeping from sorrow. Then He said to them, 'Why do you sleep? Rise and pray, lest you enter into temptation.'"

That rebuke must have made a profound impact on Peter, for many years later he wrote, "Therefore be serious and watchful in your prayers" (1 Pet. 4:7). "Watchful" means "stay alive," "stay awake," "stay alert." That is not some kind of abstract theological reasoning; Peter is talking out of his own life.

He acted too fast

Another reason Peter failed the test of loyalty is that he was impetuous. Acting without thinking was a perennial problem in Peter's life. When a group of officers from the priests and Pharisees came into the garden to take Jesus, Peter grabbed a sword and cut off the high priest's slave's ear (Luke 22:50). His motive, however, was selfishness or perhaps fear or pride, but not loyalty. Jesus rebuked him for his action and healed the man's ear.

God's will is not always easy to accept, but those who are truly loyal will be sensitive to what it is. Peter might have thought he was helping the cause of God, but he was totally oblivious to all that God was doing in Jesus' sufferings and death, and his impetuous actions actually were getting in God's way and leading to his own fall.

He followed too far away

A final reason for Peter's great failure is that he left Jesus' side and began to follow him from a distance. Luke 22:54 says, "Having arrested Him, they led Him and brought Him into the high priest's house. But Peter followed at a distance." That was perhaps the greatest disaster of all. Here was the logical consequence of all of Peter's weaknesses: cowardice. He had foolishly boasted of his willingness to die; now when he had that opportunity, Peter, for the first time in their relationship, drifted from a closeness with Jesus.

"Now when they had kindled a fire in the midst of the courtyard and sat down together, Peter sat among them" (Luke 22:55). Suddenly he was sitting in the seat of the scornful. Verse 56 states that a servant girl recognized him as a follower of Jesus and pointed him out. Peter, who had bragged so forcefully of his loyalty, now began to deny just as forcefully that he had ever known Jesus.

There he was, within sight of the Lord, denying Him, even cursing and swearing that he had never known Him (Matt. 26:72). When the rooster crowed, Jesus turned around and looked at Peter (Luke 22:61), and Peter remembered. He was so ashamed that all he could do was run away and cry his heart out (v. 62).

What about your loyalty? What have you promised Jesus? That you would love Him? That you would serve Him? That you would be faithful, always affirm Him, forsake sin, live or die for Him, witness to your neighbor? How have you done? Did you boast too much? Pray too little? Act too fast? Follow too far away? How many promises have you made to God and never kept?

It wasn't too late for Peter, and it is not too late for you. Peter finally passed the test of loyalty. He finally preached, suffered, and died for his Lord, just as he had promised. He proved himself to be a genuine disciple. The first part of his story may be sad, but beginning with the Book of Acts we can see a different Peter.

Perhaps this is the most significant thing we learn from Peter: God can turn a life around when it is finally yielded to Him. What kind of a Christian are you? Are you everything you promised Jesus Christ you would be when you first believed? Are you everything you promised Christ you would be, perhaps more recently, when you re-evaluated your life and recommitted it to Him? Are there visible, distinguishing marks that show you are a deeply committed believer?

You may lack the marks of a committed Christian, but God can transform you into a true disciple if you simply surrender and let Him have your will. The life of a committed Christian may be costly, but it is the only kind of life that really counts for eternity.

FOUR

THE SOLUTION TO A TROUBLED HEART

THOSE WERE DARK HOURS THAT NIGHT BEFORE THE LORD was betrayed, abused, tortured, and ultimately crucified. In a very short time the world of the eleven disciples was going to collapse into unbelievable chaos. Jesus, for whom they had forsaken all, was leaving. Their beloved Master, whom they loved more than life, the One whom they had been willing to die for, was going away. Their sun was about to set at midday, and their whole world was going to fall in all around them. In fact, the pains had already begun. The ramifications of all that Jesus had told the disciples must have staggered their minds, and by John 14 they were undoubtedly bewildered, perplexed, confused, and filled with anxiety.

If you have ever lost a close loved one, you know what this kind of permanent separation is like. You can only imagine the feeling of losing One who was perfect, whose fellowship was so pure, whose love was so flawless. It must have been an excruciating, horrifying pain.

Thus in the beginning of chapter 14, Jesus anticipates the sorrow of the apostles' already breaking hearts and gives them comfort upon comfort. As we read Jesus' words in the first six verses, we discover how deeply He cared for His disciples. He was about to be nailed to a cross, and He knew full well that He would soon bear the sins of the world, be cursed with the curse of God, be forsaken by His own Father, and be spit on and mocked by evil men. Any other man in that situation would have been in such a state of uncontrollable agitation that he would never have been able to focus his attention on the needs of others—but Jesus was different.

Martin Luther called this passage "the best and most comforting sermon that the Lord Christ delivered on earth, a treasure and a jewel not to be purchased with the world's goods." These verses become the foundation for comfort, not only for the eleven disciples but also for us. If you ever get to the point in your life where you think you've run out of escapes and there aren't any more places where you can rest, you'll find a tremendously soft, downy pillow in John 14:1–6:

"Let not your heart be troubled; you believe in God, believe also in Me. In My Father's house are many mansions; if it were not so, I would have told you. I go to prepare a place for you. And if I go and prepare a place for you, I will come again and receive you to Myself; that where I am, there you may be also. And where I go you know, and the way you know."

Thomas said to Him, "Lord, we do not know where You are going, and how can we know the way?"

Jesus said to him, "I am the way, the truth, and the life. No one comes to the Father except through Me."

JESUS THE TRUE COMFORTER

Here is Jesus Christ, fully divine but nevertheless totally human, anticipating the most horrible kind of experience a man would ever endure. Yet He was completely unconcerned at this point about His own experience, but wholly absorbed in the needs of His eleven friends. Surely already realizing that He was about to taste the bitter cup of death to save sinners, He nevertheless took a primary interest in the sorrows and the fears of His apostles. "Having loved His own . . . He loved them to the end" (John 13:1).

If there is a single, central message in John 14:1–6, it is that the basis of comfort is simple, trusting faith. If you're discontented, worried, anxious, bewildered, perplexed, confused, agitated, or otherwise in need of comfort, the reason is that you don't trust Christ as you should. If you really trust Him, what do you have to worry about? The reason the disciples were so stirred up is that they had begun to focus on their problems, and they didn't seem to be able to put their trust in Jesus. So in these verses He reminds them of the importance of trusting Him.

"Let not your heart be troubled" in the Greek language literally means, "Stop letting your heart be troubled." He knew the disciples were already troubled. In fact, they were probably terrified. They had been fully convinced that He was the Messiah; but the only real concept they ever had of the Messiah was as an illustrious conqueror, a kind of superhero, a sovereign ruler. Their hopes had risen even higher just a week prior, when Jesus had come riding into Jerusalem and everyone had thrown palm branches down and worshiped Him.

But even in the midst of that, Jesus had begun to talk about His dying (John 12:23–33). How could the disciples reconcile that with His Messiahship? And what about them? What kind of way was this to treat them? They had forsaken all and followed Him, and now He was going to forsake them. Not only that, but He was also going to leave them in the midst of enemies who hated Him and them. Nothing seemed to fit. What good was a Messiah who was going to die? Why would He get their hopes up, and then leave them to be hated by all men? And where were their resources going to come from?

In addition, the Lord Himself had informed the apostles that one of their own group would be the instrument of betrayal, and even that Peter, who was externally the strongest of them all, would deny Him three times that very night. Everything seemed to be unraveling in the worst way.

Yet even though the remaining eleven were wavering, their love for Him was undiminished. Perhaps in the midst of their fears they were hoping against hope that He would do something to reverse what must have seemed to them like an impossible situation. Jesus, who could read their hearts like a billboard, knew exactly what they were thinking. He was touched with the feelings of their infirmities, and, in a sense, He shared their sorrows and their hurts (cf. Heb. 4:15). They couldn't feel His pain, but He could feel theirs.

Just as Isaiah had prophesied, "In all their affliction He was afflicted" (Isa. 63:9), and, "The Lord . . . anointed [Him] to preach good tidings to the poor . . . to heal the brokenhearted . . . [and] to comfort all who mourn" (61:1–2). He indeed knew "how to speak a word in season to him who is weary" (50:4).

Interestingly, all the time He was comforting them, He knew His disciples would scatter and forsake Him later that same night. Here was the agonizing Shepherd facing the Cross, yet comforting the sheep who are going to be scattered and forsaken. "'Let not your heart be troubled; you believe in God, believe also in Me.'" (John 14:1).

WE CAN TRUST HIS PRESENCE

What our Lord is really saying in John 14:1 is, "You can trust My presence." He puts Himself on an equal plane with God: "Believe in God, believe also in Me." In the Greek, that expression can be either imperative or indicative; both forms are the same word. Therefore, He might be saying, "Believe in God and also in Me" (imperative), or "You believe in God, and you believe in Me" (indicative).

I believe, however, that Jesus was actually saying, "You believe in God, even though you can't see Him. You also believe in Me. Keep believing. Your faith in Me must not be diminished just because you will not see Me. I will still be present with you." He wanted the disciples to understand that even though He was leaving them physically,

His presence would be with them spiritually. He would be leaving, but they had always had access to God—and that would not change.

Deuteronomy 31:6 says, "Be strong and of good courage, do not fear nor be afraid of them; for the LORD your God, He is the One who goes with you. He will not leave you nor forsake you." Such faith in the omnipresence of Yahweh was a basic, implicit tenet of the Jewish religion. The Jews' history was proof of His eternal care and protection. The concept of trusting in an invisible God was nothing new to the disciples. Putting Himself on the same level as God, Jesus urged them to trust Him even when He was not physically present.

People have often misinterpreted John 14:1 to mean that Jesus was speaking of saving faith. But He was not saying the disciples should believe in Him in order to be saved; they already believed in Him. He used a linear verb form, meaning, "Keep on trusting Me. Even though I will no longer be visible, keep on trusting Me just as you are trusting God."

Unfortunately, Thomas all too often typified the disciples' early faith. After the resurrection he heard that Christ was alive and had appeared to others. Thomas' response was, "Unless I see in His hands the print of the nails, and put my finger into the print of the nails, and put my hand into His side, I will not believe" (John 20:25). Later, those were the exact conditions under which Christ met Thomas. And when he saw for himself, he believed. The other disciples were not much different. They believed what they saw, and no more. That is the lowest level of faith.

After Jesus showed Thomas the nail prints in His hands, He said, "Thomas, because you have seen Me, you have believed. Blessed are those who have not seen and yet have believed" (John 20:29). What He was trying to get across was that His visible presence was not nearly as significant as an understanding of His spiritual presence. He is there, laboring on our behalf, even when we cannot see Him. That theme influenced everything He taught them: "Lo, I am with you always, even to the end of the age" (Matt. 28:20). "I will never leave you nor forsake you" (Heb. 13:5).

Peter finally understood. Years later, he wrote in 1 Peter 1:8, speaking of Christ, "Whom having not seen you love. Though now you do not see Him, yet believing, you rejoice with joy inexpressible and full of glory." I have never seen Jesus Christ, but there is no one in existence in whom I believe more. He is alive; He is real; I know Him; I sense His presence. The Spirit of God continually witnesses in my heart about these truths.

We all live with conflict, disappointment, and pain. Most of us will experience times of deep tragedy and severe trial, but He is with us. Whatever your trouble, whatever difficulty you are in, whatever anxiety or perplexity you have, just remember the Lord Himself is there. In a way, it is better than if He were visible, because He is not hindered by the limitations of a physical body. He can be wherever we need Him. While He was here on earth, He could be in only one place at a time. Now He is available to all believers everywhere.

WE CAN TRUST HIS PROMISES

In addition to the reassurance of His constant presence, Christ gave the disciples some wonderful promises. "'In My Father's house are many mansions; if it were not so, I would have told you'" (John 14:2). That last phrase is filled with significance. He wanted them to know that He was not out to trick them, and that He would not allow them to be deceived. They had many presuppositions and misconceptions that needed to be corrected. They had believed, for example, that the Messiah would be a conquering monarch, and He taught them that first He must be a suffering servant. Their hope of eternity in heaven with Him, however, was not a misconception that needed correction. In fact, He now simply wanted to reassure them that their expectation of eternity in His kingdom was not a vain hope.

His leaving would be only to bring the fulfilment of that expectation to fruition: "I go to prepare a place for you." Can you imagine how it must have comforted them to realize for the first time why He was leaving? He wasn't going just to get away from them. He was going to get things ready for them!

It is important to note that He refers to heaven as "My Father's house." His favorite name for God was "My Father." Jesus, who had dwelt forever in the bosom of the Father, came forth so that He could reveal the Father and what the Father had been through all eternity. Now He would be glorified by death, and He was going back to full glory with the Father again in the Father's house.

In the New Testament heaven is often called a country (emphasizing its vastness), a city (because of the large number of its inhabitants), a kingdom (because of its structure and order), and a paradise (because of its beauty). But my favorite expression for heaven is "My Father's house." I remember as a child, if I went to visit relatives, or to camp, or away from home for any reason, it was an indescribable feeling of goodness to come back to my father's house. Even after I grew up and went to college, it was wonderful to have the opportunity to go home. There I was welcome. I was accepted. I was free to be myself. I could just go right in, throw my coat off, kick off my shoes, flop into a chair, and relax. It was still as much my home as my father's.

Heaven is like that. Going home to heaven will not be like going into a giant, unfamiliar palace. We will be going home. It is our Father's house, but we are residents there, not guests. It's home, not some place where we're uncomfortable. It's home like home has never been.

Translating this verse, "In my Father's house are many mansions," has for years given many people the wrong idea. Many of our songs about heaven reflect the misconception that it is full of big mansions. Some seem to think that when they arrive in heaven they'll be greeted by a heavenly real estate man, who will hand out little maps with instructions on how to get to the right mansion.

But "dwelling places" is a more accurate rendering than "mansions." In Jesus' culture, when a son was married, he seldom left his father's house. Instead, the father would simply add another wing to the existing structure. If the father had more than one son, he would attach a new wing to the house for each son's new family. The new wings would enclose a center patio, with the different families living around it.

That is the kind of arrangement John 14:2 is indicating. Jesus was not talking about tenement rooms or mansions over the hillside but rather a dwelling place that encompasses the complete family of God. We will dwell *with* God, not down the street *from* Him. We will have the same patio. And there will be enough room for everyone. There will be no overcrowding, no one turned away, no "No Vacancy" signs. Revelation 21:16 says, "The city is laid out as a square; its length is as great as its breadth. And he measured the city with the reed: twelve thousand furlongs. Its length, breadth, and height are equal." Heaven, prepared uniquely for the redeemed to inhabit in glorified bodies, will be laid out like a cube.

"Twelve thousand furlongs" (about fifteen hundred miles) squared is 2.25 million square miles. An area that size would cover almost half the continental United States. To give a point of reference, London is 140 square miles. If the ground floor of heaven were populated at the same ratio as London, it could hold a hundred billion people—far greater than the current population of our world—in their unglorified bodies, and still have plenty of room to spare. Twelve thousand furlongs cubed is 3.375 billion cubic miles, a volume larger than any of us can conceive.

Heaven is huge, but fellowship in heaven is intimate. In Revelation 21:2–3, John reports, "Then I, John, saw the holy city, New Jerusalem, coming down out of heaven from God, prepared as a bride adorned for her husband. And I heard a loud voice from heaven, saying, 'Behold, the tabernacle of God is with men, and He will dwell with them, and they shall be His people. God Himself will be with them.'" He is there, among His people dwelling with them in unbroken and unhindered fellowship.

John goes on, "And God will wipe away every tear from their eyes;

there shall be no more death, nor sorrow, nor crying. There shall be no more pain, for the former things have passed away" (v. 4). The Father takes care of all the hurts and the needs of the children in His house. There is no sense of need, no wanting anything, and no negative emotion. I already feel bound to heaven. My Father is there; my Savior is there; my home is there; my name is there; my life is there; my affections are there; my heart is there; my inheritance is there; and my citizenship is there.

Heaven will be an indescribably beautiful and glorious place. Imagine what it must be like—Jesus Christ, who created the universe in a week, has been laboring for two millennia preparing heaven to be the habitation of His people. Revelation 21:18–22 describes it:

> The construction of its wall was of jasper; and the city was pure gold, like clear glass. The foundations of the wall of the city were adorned with all kinds of precious stones: the first foundation was jasper, the second sapphire, the third chalcedony, the fourth emerald, the fifth sardonyx, the sixth sardius, the seventh chrysolite, the eighth beryl, the ninth topaz, the tenth chrysoprase, the eleventh jacinth, and the twelfth amethyst. The twelve gates were twelve pearls: each individual gate was of one pearl. And the street of the city was pure gold, like transparent glass. But I saw no temple in it, for the Lord God Almighty and the Lamb are its temple.

John goes on to write of how the glory of God will illuminate the city. Imagine the purest, brightest light flashing through the magnificent jewels in the walls. Its gates are never shut (v. 25), yet nothing defiling can enter it. What a city it will be! Transparent gold, diamond walls, and light from the Lamb's glory will form a spectacle of dazzling beauty. And the Lord Jesus is preparing it especially for His own.

"'If it were not so, I would have told you'" (John 14:2). Jesus is saying, "Trust my promises! I've always told you the truth." He continues,

"'And if I go and prepare a place for you, I will come again and receive you to Myself; that where I am, there you may be also'" (v. 3). What a reassurance those words must have been to the frightened disciples that dark night. As surely as Jesus was leaving, He would return again, in person, to receive them personally into the place He would prepare for them.

We can have complete confidence that He is coming back, although we do not know when. In fact, Jesus is eager to return and claim His own. In John 17:24, He prays to the Father, "I desire that they also whom You gave Me may be with Me where I am, that they may behold My glory." Jesus wants us with Him as much as we want to be with Him.

The truth of Jesus' second coming is on the lips of Christians all over the world. It always has been. But today there seems to be a heightened awareness, a deepening anticipation that Jesus could well come in this generation. In fact, He could come today. But even if He does not, we know He will return some day.

WE CAN TRUST HIS PERSON

The disciples must have been completely bewildered when Jesus, speaking of His departure, added, "'And where I go you know, and the way you know'" (John 14:4). Up to this point, they had completely resisted any idea of His leaving at all. Now they weren't certain of anything. Thomas probably spoke for the rest, "'Lord, we do not know where You are going, and how can we know the way?'" (v. 5).

Thomas was saying, "Our knowledge stops at death. How can we go to the Father unless we die? You're going to die and go somewhere, but we don't know what's going on after death. We don't have any maps on how to get to the Father after You die." It was a good question.

Jesus' response is profound: "'I am the way, the truth, and the life. No one comes to the Father except through Me'" (v. 6). In other words, "You don't need to know how to get there. I'm coming to get

56

you." It is a reaffirmation of all He had just promised them. It's a beautiful promise. Have you ever been driving in an unfamiliar town and stopped to ask directions? If your experience is like mine, you've probably had someone give you a complex set of directions that you could not possibly understand. How much better it would be for the person to say, "Follow me; I'll take you there."

That's what Jesus does. He doesn't merely give us the directions to the Father's house—He carries us there. That's why death for the Christian is such a glorious experience. Whether we die or He takes us in the Rapture, we know we can trust Him to take us to the Father's house.

Augustus Toplady, who wrote "Rock of Ages," died in London at the age of 38. When death drew near, he said, "It is my dying vow that these great and glorious truths which the Lord in rich mercy has given me to believe and enabled me to preach are now brought into practical and heartfelt experience. They are the very joy and support of my soul. The comfort flowing from them carries me far above the things of time and sin." Then he said, "Had I wings like a dove, I would fly away to the bosom of God and be at rest." About an hour before he died, he seemed to awaken from a gentle slumber, and his last words were, "O, what delight! Who can fathom the joys of heaven! I know it cannot be long now until my Savior will come for me." And then bursting into a flood of tears he said, "All is light, light, light, light, the brightness of His own glory. O, come Lord Jesus, come! Come quickly!" And he closed his eyes.

In effect, Jesus says, "Trust Me. You don't need a map; I'm the way, the truth, and the life. I am the way to the Father. I am the truth, whether in this world or the world to come. I am the life that is eternal."

Christ is everything a man or woman needs. Everything that Adam lost we may regain in Jesus Christ. We can trust His presence, His promises, and His person, for He is the way, the truth, and the life. I know of no greater comfort in all the world than that.

FIVE

JESUS IS GOD

THE STRATEGIC IMPORTANCE OF JESUS' FINAL HOURS IN THE upper room with His eleven remaining disciples cannot be over-stated. All His instructions to them that night—His warnings, His teaching, His commandments, His promises, and His revelation—were calculated to strengthen them spiritually and brace them for the trauma they were about to experience. It was essential that Jesus prepare them for the shock of His death. The news of His leaving was a tremendous blow to them, and their hearts were already deeply troubled. They had put all their faith in Him, and they loved Him more than life itself. Their faith might have been seriously damaged if they had seen Him die with-out hearing what He had to say in those few remaining hours.

The disciples had been witnesses to some amazing events in the three brief years of Jesus' ministry. He had cast out demons, healed people with every conceivable sickness, and even raised people from the dead. He had demonstrated His power over every adversary, and in every situation where it seemed He was threatened, He had come forth the victor. He had successfully countered every argument, answered every question, resisted every temptation, and confounded every enemy. But now He was predicting His own death at the hands of wicked men.

The confused disciples did not understand how Messiah could become a victim of the people. It didn't fit their concept of what His mission would be. Not only that, but they had also become increasingly aware that Jesus was the incarnation of God. They thought of Him as invincible, omniscient, and devoid of any kind of weakness. Now they were understandably confused. Why would He die? How can He die? Who could defeat Him? How could anyone else ever accept Him as Messiah if He died? Did this mean that all they had lived for during the past three years was in vain? And most crucial of all, did it mean that Jesus was not who they thought He was?

Jesus, sensing the nagging questions of their troubled hearts, continued His ministry of comfort to them by reaffirming His deity:

> "If you had known Me, you would have known My Father also; and from now on you know Him and have seen Him."
>
> Philip said to Him, "Lord, show us the Father, and it is sufficient for us."
>
> Jesus said to him, "Have I been with you so long, and yet you have not known Me, Philip? He who has seen Me has seen the Father; so how can you say, 'Show us the Father'? Do you not believe that I am in the Father, and the Father in Me? The words that I speak to you I do not speak on My own authority; but the Father who dwells in Me does the works. Believe Me that I am in the Father and the Father in Me, or else believe Me for the sake of the works themselves.
>
> "Most assuredly, I say to you, he who believes in Me, the works that I do he will do also; and greater works than these he will do, because I go to My Father. And whatever you ask in My name, that I will do, that the Father may be glorified in the Son. If you ask anything in My name, I will do it." (John 14:7–14)

The implications of Jesus' words in those few verses are overwhelming. The fact that He claims to be God is profound enough. But then He adds a guarantee that believers in Him would have power to do even greater works than He had done, and concludes by saying that if we ask anything in His name He will do it. These words are monumental in declaring not only who Jesus is, but also what He intends to do in and for those who belong to Him.

And the passage contains three momentous revelations to His disciples and us: the revelation of His person, the revelation of His power, and the revelation of His promise.

THE REVELATION OF HIS PERSON

Only a few days before, when Jesus had entered Jerusalem on the back of a donkey to shouts of "Hosanna!" there was no question in the disciples' minds about who He was. Now they weren't so sure. In their hearts they were asking questions about Him that had been answered before. Therefore Jesus reiterated to them who He really was, by revealing His person to them in fresh and unmistakable terminology: "'He who has seen Me has seen the Father'" (v. 9). "'I am in the Father and the Father in Me'" (v. 10).

What did He reveal to them about Himself? One thing: that He is God. They had heard His claims of deity before, and they had witnessed the proof of it in His works. He had just said that He was the way to God, the truth about God, in the very life of God (v. 6). He goes a step further in verses 7–10 and says in unequivocal terms that He is God. His words must have been staggering, because the claim is so tremendous.

No fair-minded person will simply dismiss Jesus' claim to be God. The single, central, most important issue of all about Jesus is the question of His deity. Everyone who studies the life of Jesus must confront the issue, because of what the New Testament teaches. Some conclude that Jesus was a madman, who had delusions of grandeur. Others believe He was a fraud. Still others try to say He was only a good teacher, but that is not really an option, because good teachers don't claim to be God. Either He was God in the flesh, or He was a madman, or a fraud. Regarding these options, Christian essayist C. S. Lewis rightly observed that "the one thing we must not say" about Jesus is that He is "a great moral teacher" but not God. Lewis further noted:

> A man who was merely a man and said the sort of things Jesus said would not be a great moral teacher. He would either be a lunatic—on a level with the man who says he is a poached egg—or else he would be the Devil of Hell. You must make your choice. Either this man was, and is, the Son of God: or else a madman or something worse. (*Mere Christianity* [New York: Macmillan, 1960], 41)

Sabellius, a second-century heretic and the forerunner of the Unitarian sect, taught that Jesus was only a radiation, a manifestation of God. But He is *not* merely a manifestation of God; He *is* God manifest. There is a significant difference. Jesus is uniquely one with, but distinct from, the Father—God evident in human flesh.

In John 14:7–10 Jesus makes the very simple, undisguised claim that He is no less than God Himself. He had told the apostles many times in the past that He proceeded from the Father. His comment in verse 4 implies that they should have understood: "Where I go you know, and the way you know." They should have at least known that He was going to be with the Father. But Jesus' words left them scratching their heads, and Thomas asked for an explanation. Jesus' answer was simply, "'I am the way, the truth, and the life. No one comes to the Father except through Me'" (v. 6).

It was a claim of divine authority. In other words, "If you know Me, you know the way to get where I'm going. I'm going to the Father, and I'll take you." He reinforced that claim with mild rebuke for their unbelief and a reassurance that they were as secure in their relationship with the Father as they were in their relationship with the Son: "'If you had known Me, you would have known My Father also; and from now on you know Him and have seen Him'" (v. 7).

In a sense, the disciples did not know Jesus at all. If they had really known Him, they wouldn't have been worried about where the Father was.

They had some knowledge of who Jesus was. They had declared that He was Messiah, the Anointed One of God. Peter had even made the statement that He was the Son of the living God (Matt. 16:16). They were very close to grasping fully the truth of His deity and beginning to understand the meaning of it. Nevertheless, they were still confused, so Jesus stated it in the clearest possible language, in terms they could not possibly miss: "'If you had known Me, you would have known My Father also; and from now on you know Him and have seen Him. . . . He who has seen Me has seen the Father. . . . I am in the Father, and the Father in Me'" (vv. 7–10).

Jesus was telling His disciples, "If you really knew Me in depth, you would know the Father also. Your confusion about the Father means that there must be some gaps in your knowledge of Me." If they had really seen Jesus fully as God, they would not have had fears, doubts, and questions about who the Father was and how to get to Him.

Remember, Jesus' words were meant to comfort them. They knew He loved them. He wanted them to know that God cared for them in the same way, because He and the Father are one. To have a relationship with one is to have a relationship with the other. That is an important, eternal principle. If you reject the Son, you have rejected the Father; and if you receive the Son, you have received the Father. The Apostle John grasped this in its fullness, and it became a theme of his ministry. Years later, he wrote, "Whoever denies the Son does not have the Father either; he who acknowledges the Son has the Father also" (1 John 2:23).

But it appears that none of the disciples immediately understood the full import of what Jesus was telling them. His words, "'From now on you know Him and have seen Him'" (v. 7) are more a prediction than a proclamation. "From now on" does not mean "from this precise moment on," because Jesus knew they did not yet grasp what He was saying. (In fact, verse 8 reveals Philip still didn't fully know who Jesus was.)

Similarly, "You know Him and have seen Him" does not mean the disciples now completely understood who God was and is. Jesus, using the idiom of His day, spoke in the present tense to signify the ultimate certainty of what He was saying. The message to the disciples is, "Starting now, you are going to begin to understand." Through the events of the next forty days—the death of Jesus Christ, His resurrection, His ascension and the coming Holy Spirit—they would come to understand more fully about Jesus' person and His relationship to the Father.

And that is exactly what happened. Thomas, for example, had doubted the Resurrection even after hearing eyewitness testimony. But when he saw Christ, it all fell into place—finally—and he understood who Jesus was. He looked at the risen Lord and Savior and said, "'My Lord and my God!'" (John 20:28).

Philip's request in John 14:8, "'Lord, show us the Father, and it is sufficient for us,'" proved that the disciples, during their time in the upper room, did not see the full truth of who Jesus is. It was a shallow, faithless, ignorant thing to say, and it revealed that Philip's knowledge of God was incomplete. So he did what people have done throughout history: He asked to see.

Philip was trying to walk by sight rather than by faith. It wasn't enough for him to believe; he wanted to see something. It could be that he remembered the account of Exodus 33, when Moses was tucked behind a rock and saw the afterglow of God's glory pass by. Or maybe he recalled the words of Isaiah 40:5: "The glory of the LORD shall be revealed, and all flesh shall see it together."

Perhaps, but I don't think Philip was a biblical scholar at all. Clearly he was a faithless disciple who wanted sight to substitute for faith. We can understand his feelings. It would be a lot easier to tolerate Jesus' departure if the disciples could first have a glimpse of the Father, just to make certain He really knew where He was going. It would be much easier to cling to Jesus' promise that He would come again to get them, if God could come and confirm it. If Jesus could do that, there would be no doubt about the validity of His claims. God Himself would be a guarantee that Jesus' pledge was secure.

It wasn't the first time Jesus had dealt with this same question. In John 8:19, the apostle records, "Then they [some unbelieving Jews] said to Him, 'Where is Your Father?' Jesus answered, 'You know neither Me nor My Father. If you had known Me, you would have known My Father also.'"

Philip's question revealed his lack of faith, and Jesus gave him the same answer He had given the unbelieving Jews. "Jesus said to him, 'Have I been with you so long, and yet you have not known Me, Philip? He who has seen Me has seen the Father; so how can you say, "Show us the Father"?'" (14:9). That was, of course, a rebuke to Philip, but I believe there was also pathos in the voice of Jesus. Can you imagine the heartbreak of Jesus after He had poured His life into these twelve men for three years, to know that one of them was a traitor, one of them a profane denier, and the other ten men of little faith? It was the night before His death, and they still didn't really know who He was.

Imagine Philip, standing there staring Christ in the face and asking Him to show him God. Jesus' answer to him was, "Open your eyes. You've been looking at Me for three years." They who had seen Jesus had seen the visible manifestation of God. The writer of Hebrews says, "[Jesus Christ is] the brightness of His glory and the express image of His person" (Heb. 1:3). The Apostle Paul declares, "He is the image of the invisible God" (Col. 1:15), and "In Him dwells all the fullness of the Godhead bodily" (2:9). Jesus is God.

It is easy to see how unbelievers might say what Philip did. But for him to ask to see the Father as proof of Jesus' claims doesn't make much sense. He and the other disciples had seen Jesus' works and heard His words for three years.

Anyone who has ever discipled a newer believer must know something of Jesus' frustration in the face of Philip's unbelief. But Jesus was not discouraged; He had gone as far as He could with the disciples, and now He was ready to turn them over to the Holy Spirit. That is a good principle to apply in discipleship.

Jesus' answer might not have seemed very satisfying to Philip, but it was exactly what Philip needed. Jesus didn't do any miracles for him or give him any great display of power; He simply commanded him to believe. "'Do you not believe that I am in the Father, and the Father in Me? The words that I speak to you I do not speak on My own authority; but the Father who dwells in Me does the works. Believe Me that I am in the Father and the Father in Me, or else believe Me for the sake of the works themselves'" (John 14:10–11). Philip asked for sight; Jesus told him to seek faith instead.

Christianity is all about believing. If you think the height of spirituality is to see miracles, hear the voice of God booming out of the ceiling, or experience various supernatural phenomena, you don't have a clue regarding what believing God is really all about. Satan can duplicate all those things in counterfeit. If you want manifestations or supernatural power, you can get them at a seance.

Christianity is walking by faith, not sight. I have never seen Jesus, never had a vision, never seen angelic hosts, never heard heavenly voices, and never been carried into the third heaven. Yet my spiritual eyes can see things that my physical eyes could never even conceive of. I don't want visions, miracles, and strange phenomena. I want one thing—I want what the disciples prayed for in Luke 17:5: "Increase our faith."

Faith is not as one little boy described it: "Believing in something you know ain't so." In fact, faith is just the opposite—believing in something you know *is* so. Genuine faith has an essential basis in fact.

The disciples certainly had a factual basis for their faith, and Jesus reemphasized that to Philip: "'The words that I speak to you I do not speak on My own authority; but the Father who dwells in Me does the works. Believe Me that I am in the Father and the Father in Me, or else believe Me for the sake of the works themselves'" (John 14:10–11). If Philip and the others had truly been listening for the past three years, if they had really paid attention to the works Jesus did, they would not have doubted now.

There is always a danger of doubting in the darkness things that we have seen clearly in the light. That's what the disciples were doing. During the three years of Jesus' earthly ministry they had repeatedly heard and seen proof that He was God incarnate. Now their faith was wavering, in spite of the solid, factual foundation upon which it was built. They had heard all His claims, all His teachings, all His insights probing into hidden truths, all His words revealing a supernatural knowledge of the human heart. He had already answered all their deepest, most heartfelt questions, even the ones not articulated out loud. And if His words were not sufficient proof, they had seen His works—His miracles and His sinless life.

Philip's request to see God, then, was a gross display of unbelief. He didn't need to see anything; Jesus had proved His deity. What more could He show the disciples? He was God manifest. In addition to observing His words and works, they had experienced His love for them. Therefore, at this point, how could one of them possibly ask to see God?

And so He reaffirmed to the eleven the tremendous revelation that He is God. If they could grasp that truth, they could rest easy, knowing they were secure.

THE REVELATION OF HIS POWER

Next, He revealed to them the incredible resource of power they had available through Him. "'Most assuredly, I say to you, he who believes in Me, the works that I do he will do also; and greater works than these he will do, because I go to My Father'" (John 14:12). Christians over the centuries have wondered at the richness of such a promise. What does it mean? How could anyone do greater works than Jesus had done? He had healed people blind from birth, cast out the most powerful demons, and even raised a man (Lazarus) from the dead after four days. What could possibly be greater than those miracles?

The key to understanding this promise is in the last phrase of verse 12: "because I go to My Father." When Jesus went to the Father, He sent the Holy Spirit. He completely transformed the disciples from a group of fearful, timid individuals into a cohesive force that reached the world with the gospel. The impact of their preaching exceeded even the impact of Jesus' preaching during His lifetime. Jesus had never preached outside Palestine. Within His lifetime Europe had never received the word of the gospel, but under the ministry of the disciples it began to spread, and it's still spreading today. Their works were greater than His, not in power, but in scope. Through the indwelling Holy Spirit, each one of those disciples had access to power in dimensions they did not previously have, even with the physical presence of Christ.

The disciples undoubtedly thought that without Christ they would be reduced to nothing. He was the source of their strength; how could they have power without Him? His promise was meant to ease those fears. If they felt secure in His presence, they would be even more secure, more powerful, able to do more, if He returned to the Father and sent the Holy Spirit.

The disciples had power to work great miracles. Acts 5:12, 15 says that "through the hands of the apostles many signs and wonders were done among the people. . . . they brought the sick out into the streets and laid them on beds and couches, that at least the shadow of Peter passing by might fall on some of them."

Acts 2:40–41 records that Peter preached and three thousand people were saved. That never happened during the ministry of Jesus. He never saw widespread revival. The gospel never went to the Gentiles while He was on earth, but through the works of His apostles after He departed, conversions took place everywhere.

And after all, the greatest miracle God can perform is salvation. Every time we introduce someone to faith in Jesus Christ, we are observers of the new birth; we are supporting the most important spiritual work in the world. How exciting it is to be involved in what God is doing spiritually and to do things greater than even Jesus saw in His day.

THE REVELATION OF HIS PROMISE

Finally, Jesus gave the apostles a promise meant to ease the grief they felt at His leaving: "'And whatever you ask in My name, that I will do, that the Father may be glorified in the Son. If you ask anything in My name, I will do it'" (John 14:13–14).

Jesus had fed them. He had helped them catch their fish. On one occasion He had even provided Peter's tax money out of the mouth of a fish. He had supplied all their needs, but now He was leaving, and they must have wondered, *How are we going to get a job? How are we going to fit back into society? What will we do without Him?*

Jesus' disciples had left everything and were completely without resources. Without their Master they would be all alone in a hostile world. Yet, He assured them, they did not need to worry about any of their needs. The gap between Him and them would be closed instantly whenever they prayed. Even though He would be absent, they would have access to all His supplies.

That is not carte blanche for every whim of the flesh. There's a qualifying statement repeated twice. He doesn't say, "I'll give you *absolutely anything* you ask for," but rather, "I'll do what you ask *in My name.*" That does not mean we can simply tack "in-Jesus'-name-amen" on the end of our prayers and expect the answers we want every time. Neither is it a special formula or "abracadabra" to use to get wishes granted.

The name of Jesus stands for all that He is. Throughout Scripture, God's names are the same as His attributes. When Isaiah prophesied that Messiah would be called "Wonderful, Counselor, Mighty God, Everlasting Father, Prince of Peace" (9:6), he was not giving Him actual names, but rather an overview of Messiah's character. "I AM WHO I AM," the name revealed to Moses in Exodus 3:14, is as much an affirmation of God's eternal nature as it is a name by which He is to be called.

Therefore praying in the name of Jesus is more than merely mentioning His name at the end of our prayers. If we truly pray in Jesus' name, we can pray only for that which is consistent with His perfect character, and for that which will bring glory to Him. It implies an acknowledgment of all that He has done and a submission to His will.

What praying in Jesus' name really means is that we should pray as if our Lord Himself were doing the asking. We approach the throne of the Father in full identification with the Son, seeking only what He would seek. When we pray with that perspective, we begin to pray for the things that really matter, and we eliminate selfish requests.

His promise when we pray that way is, "I will do it" (John 14:14). That is a guarantee that, within His will, we cannot lack anything. His concern for His own transcends all circumstances, so that "neither death nor life, nor angels nor principalities nor powers, nor things present nor things to come, nor height nor depth, nor any other created thing, shall be able to separate us from the love of God which is in Christ Jesus our Lord" (Rom. 8:38–39).

John 14:13–14 is the heart of Jesus' message of comfort to His terrified disciples, and it must have been tremendously reassuring to hear those words and ponder them. In the midst of the collapse of their dreams and hopes, He gave them Himself as the Rock to which they could cling and under which they could seek shelter.

Jesus Christ cares no less for those who are His disciples today. His promises are still valid; His power has not diminished; and His person is unchanging. We do not have the benefit of His physical presence, but we have His Holy Spirit. And although we cannot see Jesus, we can sense His love for us as the Spirit sheds it abroad in our hearts. In many ways, we know Him better than if we knew Him from His physical presence. As the Apostle Peter encourages us, "Whom having not seen you love. Though now you do not see Him, yet believing, you rejoice with joy inexpressible and full of glory" (1 Pet. 1:8).

What a thrill it is to experience His love in this way, and what a comfort to know that He is God, and He cares for us.

SIX

THE HOLY SPIRIT COMES TO COMFORT

You cannot study the New Testament long without realizing that there is a dichotomy between what we as Christians are responsible to do and what God has already done on our behalf. To understand the distinction is to get a grip on the basics of our faith.

On the one hand, we are told repeatedly in Scripture how we are to live, act, think, and speak. We are enjoined to be this or to refrain from that. We are informed about what we are to do, at what point we are to commit ourselves, and for what tasks we are to separate ourselves. All of that is essential to our Christian faith.

But on the other hand, much of the New Testament emphasizes what Christ has already done for us. We are told that we are called, justified, sanctified, and kept in the faith through no effort of our own. We learn that Christ and the Holy Spirit are continually interceding on our behalf. And we discover that we are the recipients of an inheritance that cannot be measured in human terms.

Most of Jesus' final discourse to His disciples consists not of commandments they were responsible to obey, but rather of promises concerning what He would do for them. John 14:15–26 is the heart of His message of comfort. Here, Jesus gives to His disciples the promise that after His departure, the Holy Spirit would come in His place:

"If you love Me, keep My commandments. And I will pray the Father, and He will give you another Helper, that He may abide with you forever—the Spirit of truth, whom the world cannot receive, because it neither sees Him nor knows Him; but you know Him, for He dwells with you and will be in you. I will not leave you orphans; I will come to you. A little while longer and the world will see Me no more, but you will see Me. Because I live, you will live also. At that day you will know that I am in My Father, and you in Me, and I in you. He who has My commandments and keeps them, it is he who loves Me. And he who loves Me will be loved by My Father, and I will love him and manifest Myself to him."

Judas (not Iscariot) said to Him, "Lord, how is it that You will manifest Yourself to us, and not to the world?"

Jesus answered and said to him, "If anyone loves Me, he will keep My word; and My Father will love him, and We will come to him and make Our home with him. He who does not love Me does not keep My words; and the word which you hear is not Mine but the Father's who sent Me. These things I have spoken to you while being present with you. But the Helper, the Holy Spirit, whom the Father will send in My name, He will teach you all things, and bring to your remembrance all things that I said to you."

The promises Jesus makes in that brief passage are staggering. To whom does He make them? In context, Jesus is speaking to His eleven disciples, but the scope of His promises is broader than that. Verse 15 says, "'If you love Me, keep My commandments.'" Implied in that statement is the corollary that the following promises apply to all those who love Jesus Christ. Thus they apply to all believers in Christ, those whose faith and obedience characterizes their love for Him.

We cannot miss Jesus' clear statement here that the proof of genuine love for Him is obedience to His commandments. Later in this passage Jesus twice repeats His command. "'He who has My commandments and keeps them, it is he who loves Me. And he who loves Me will be loved by My Father, and I will love him and manifest Myself to him'" (v. 21). "'If anyone loves Me, he will keep My word . . . He who does not love Me does not keep My words'" (vv. 23–24). Elsewhere the New Testament repeats this truth a number of times (cf. Matt. 7:21; 10:22; Luke 11:28; Rom. 6:17; 2 Cor. 10:5; Phil. 2:13–14; James 1:25; 2:14–20).

Love for Christ is not sentimentalism or a sickly pseudospiritual poignant attitude, and it does not result in mere lip service. Real love for Him is demonstrated by an active, eager, joyful, responsive obedience to His commandments. What you say about your love for Him is relatively unimportant—what counts is that you demonstrate your love for Him by how you live your life. Discipleship is not singing songs and saying nice things. True discipleship is obedience.

To those who are obedient, the Lord extends a number of promises. These promises are for all disciples from all time periods since Christ ascended. They are benefits God has provided us without any effort on our part. All of them are tied to the coming of the Holy Spirit, the Comforter, Teacher, and Helper who would minister to the disciples when Jesus left. Together, these promises constitute a legacy left by our Lord to all those who love Him.

THE INDWELLING SPIRIT

The promise of the Holy Spirit is the culmination of all that Jesus had to say to comfort His eleven troubled disciples. In that hour of turmoil, they feared being left alone. Jesus assured them that they would not be left to fend for themselves, but they would have a supernatural Helper. The Greek word for "Helper" is *parakletos,* which literally means "one who is called *[kaleo]* alongside *[para].*" We sometimes use the term *paraclete* in English. (The King James Bible translates it

"Comforter," which is another one of the meanings of the word.) Jesus is saying, "I am going to send a Helper, a Comforter—One to stand alongside you."

The Greek word translation of "another" is crucial to an understanding of Jesus' meaning. The Greek language, with all its complexities, is much more precise than English. The Greeks had two words that meant "another." One was *heteros,* which means "another kind," as in, "This wrench doesn't fit; bring me another one." *Allos* also means "another," but it means "another of the same kind," as in "I enjoyed that sandwich; I think I'll have another."

Allos is the word Jesus used to describe the Holy Spirit: "another [*allos*] Helper." He is, in effect, saying, "I am sending you One of exactly the same essence as Me." The disciples would have known His meaning immediately. He was not sending just any old helper, but One exactly like Himself, with the same compassion, the same attributes of deity, and the same love for them.

Jesus had been their *Paraclete* for three years. He had helped them, comforted them, and walked alongside them. Now they would have another Helper—One exactly like Jesus—to minister to them as He had.

The Holy Spirit is not a mystical power or force; He is a person as much as Jesus is a person. He is not a floating fog or some kind of ghostlike emanation. It is unfortunate that the King James translators used the term "Ghost" instead of "Spirit" to translate the Greek *pneuma.* For generations people have had the erroneous idea that the Holy Spirit is something like the comic-book character Casper, the friendly ghost. However, He is not a ghost, but a person.

All believers have two *paracletes*—the Spirit of God within us, and Christ at the right hand of the Father in heaven. First John 2:1 says, "My little children, these things I write to you, so that you may not sin. And if anyone sins, we have an Advocate with the Father, Jesus Christ the righteous." The word that translated to "Advocate" in that verse is *parakletos.*

You can imagine the disciples must have been greatly encouraged and comforted to hear Jesus say He would send another Helper like Him to minister to them in His place after He ascended. As One who possesses exactly the same divine essence as Christ, the Holy Spirit would be a perfect substitute for Jesus' familiar presence.

But our Lord's promise extended beyond that. His words in John 14:16 beautifully culminate the message of comfort: "that He may abide with you forever." Not only would the Holy Spirit come to dwell with them—He would never leave. Once the Spirit of God resides within a person, He is there forever.

In Luke 11:13, Jesus told His disciples that the Father would give them the Holy Spirit if they asked. Yet here, before they can even ask, He asks in their behalf. That is a good picture of how our prayers operate. The Lord knows what we have need of before we even ask. I'm sure that often, before we get our prayers organized, Christ has already presented those needs to the Father. That is part of His ministry of advocacy and intercession.

SPIRITUAL PERCEPTION

Notice that the Spirit is called "the Spirit of truth." He is both the essence of truth, because He is God, and the One who guides us into all truth. In fact, unsaved people do not recognize the Spirit or His work, and that is as Jesus said it would be: "'The Spirit of truth, whom the world cannot receive, because it neither sees Him nor knows Him'" (John 14:17). If the world didn't recognize the first Comforter, Jesus, you cannot expect it to recognize the second One, who is exactly like the first.

Unregenerate people have no facility for perception. They have no way to see the working of the power of the Holy Spirit. When the academic minds of Jesus' day came to their conclusion about who He was, their very astute, reasoned, theological pronouncement was that He was from the devil (Matt. 12:24)—and that came after several years of studying His ministry. That shows graphically the spiritual capacity of the unregenerate. Given all the facts, such people will invariably conclude the wrong thing.

In 1 Corinthians 2:12–14, the Apostle Paul writes,

Now we have received, not the spirit of the world, but the Spirit who is from God, that we might know the things that have been freely given to us by God.

These things we also speak, not in words which man's wisdom teaches but which the Holy Spirit teaches, comparing spiritual things with spiritual. But the natural man does not receive the things of the Spirit of God, for they are foolishness to him; nor can he know them, because they are spiritually discerned.

In other words, the only way a person can understand the things of God is to have the Spirit of God. The natural man cannot understand the Holy Spirit's work.

In fact, Jesus indicted the Jewish leaders for clinging to their natural understanding of spiritual matters:

"You are of your father the devil, and the desires of your father you want to do. He was a murderer from the beginning, and does not stand in the truth, because there is no truth in him. When he speaks a lie, he speaks from his own resources, for he is a liar and the father of it. But because I tell the truth, you do not believe Me. . . . He who is of God hears God's words; therefore you do not hear, because you are not of God." (John 8:44–45, 47)

As unsaved men, they had no capacity to comprehend the truth of God.

So Jesus told His disciples that when the Holy Spirit came, the people of the world would not get the message, anymore than they believed Him when He came. And He was right. In Acts 2, when the

Holy Spirit came on the day of Pentecost, the unbelievers who witnessed the manifestation thought the disciples were drunk. The Holy Spirit was just as foreign to the stubborn, rejecting world as Jesus had been.

When I first studied John 14, I was puzzled about why in that context Jesus told the disciples the world would not respond to the Holy Spirit. Then it became clear that with all the promises Jesus was giving them, they might have succumbed to overconfidence. He had told them they would do greater things than even He had done (v. 12), and He had promised to answer every prayer they asked (v. 14). If the Lord had not placed things into a complete perspective beforehand, the apostles, with their confidence so high, might have been totally deflated when they first encountered rejection. Jesus was simply trying to give them a tempered, balanced response.

THE ETERNAL UNION WITH GOD

At the end of John 14:17, our Lord reaffirms a classic biblical truth: "'But you know Him [the Holy Spirit], for He dwells with you and will be in you.'" The disciples knew of the ministry of God's Spirit from the Old Testament. In that economy, the Spirit functioned in certain distinct roles (creation, empowerment) and in other ways (revelation, regeneration, and preservation) that foreshadowed His ministry in the New Testament. (The Spirit's role differed from Old to New Covenant, but His essential person and character remained the same. For a complete discussion of the Spirit's person and work in the Old Testament, see chapter 2, "The Spirit in the Old Testament," in my *The Silent Shepherd* [Wheaton, Ill.: Victor Books, 1996]). At Jesus' baptism the Holy Spirit had descended on Him like a dove. So the disciples were not ignorant of the Spirit's ministry.

But Jesus' words at the end of verse 17 indicate that from then on something new was coming in His ministry. The Holy Spirit would not just be present with the disciples as before, but He would indwell them, and the verb tense in the Greek indicates that it would be a permanent, uninterrupted residence.

What a privilege it is in the grace of God that He would plant His very essence in us. Every moment of our existence throughout all eternity, we have the presence of the Holy Spirit not just with us but also within us (cf. John 7:37–39; Acts 2:1–4; 19:1–7; 1 Cor. 12:11–13).

THE PRESENCE OF CHRIST

Our Lord expands the promise in John 14:18–19: "'I will not leave you orphans; I will come to you. A little while longer and the world will see Me no more, but you will see Me.'" This is the picture of a dying father. He would literally die before another day had passed, and He wanted to reassure the disciples that they could nevertheless count on His presence after that.

There are at least two elements involved in this promise. For one thing, Christ was guaranteeing His followers that He would rise from the dead. His dying on the cross would not be the end of existence. But beyond that, He promised, "I will come to you." Some say that this is a promise of the rapture. But if this verse referred to the rapture, it would say, "I will come *for* you." Others say it is only a promise that the disciples would see Him after the resurrection. I don't think that's the best interpretation either, because He was on earth for only forty days after He arose. That seems like a small amount of comfort.

I believe Jesus is here speaking of His spiritual presence in every believer through the agency of the Holy Spirit. He is saying, "When the Spirit of God comes to reside in your life, I will be there as well." In Matthew 28:20, He promises, "'Lo, I am with you always, even to the end of the age.'"

This is the mystery of the Trinity: the Holy Spirit abides in us (John 14:17), Christ indwells us (Col. 1:27), and God is in us (1 John 4:12). This presence is the source of eternal life. Jesus goes on to say, "Because I live, you will live also" (John 14:19).

How is it that a person can sense the presence of God within him? How can he know the Spirit is there? How can he know that Christ lives within? He must be spiritually alive to have spiritual perception. The spiritually dead individual understands nothing about God. He cannot respond to God.

But the person who is spiritually alive lives in another dimension. He is alive to the spiritual world. And the basis of his life is the resurrection of Jesus Christ: "Because I live, you will live also." Eternal life isn't the quantity of life; it's the kind of life that makes you eternally sensitive to what God is doing. Here is the essence of spiritual life: to be alive spiritually, walking with God, sensing the Holy Spirit, communing with Christ, and moving and participating in the spiritual realm. The world cannot know anything about that.

FULL UNDERSTANDING

Those who love Christ are not only indwelt by the Holy Spirit, Christ, and the Father, but also enjoy a supernatural union with the members of the Trinity. Jesus illustrates this union by comparing it with His relationship to the Father: "'At that day you will know that I am in My Father, and you in Me, and I in you'" (John 14:20). We are one with God and Christ. That's why sin is so out of place in the believer's life.

It is confusing to try to understand how we can be at the same time in Christ and He in us. It doesn't seem logical, but it's not supposed to be. We are so closely united spiritually with our Lord that the distinctions are difficult to sort out. And we won't understand them until we reach heaven.

The disciples still did not understand the mystery of the relation of the Son to the Father. Union with deity was such a foreign concept to them that their minds could not conceive of it. So Jesus told them, "In that day you will know." It seems clear that He was referring to the day of Pentecost, in which the Holy Spirit came. Before the Spirit came to dwell within them and teach them the truth, they had no way of understanding the relationship of God with Christ and how it corresponded to their relationship with Him.

But as suddenly as they received the Holy Spirit in Acts 2, they began to understand. Peter is probably the best evidence of that. Brash, denying Peter, who rarely seemed to understand anything, stood up on the very day that the Spirit of God came to dwell within him and preached a powerful sermon, clearly delineating exactly who Jesus Christ is, who the Father is, why He rose, and what it all meant in reference to Israel.

Peter had not secretly acquired a seminary education, or read all the good theology books—those things weren't even available. The Spirit of God had supernaturally untangled Peter's previous confusion, and everything had fallen into place for him. It may not have made any more sense logically than it did before, but in a spiritual sense, he understood.

THE MANIFESTATION OF THE FATHER

In a beautiful summary, crushing the full bloom of redemption into one little wisp of fragrance, Jesus reviews how a man comes into that supernatural union with Him: "'He who has My commandments and keeps them, it is he who loves Me. And he who loves Me will be loved by My Father, and I will love him and manifest Myself to him'" (John 14:21). He has come full circle to the point at which He began in verse 15.

The Father wants to glorify the Son, and He continually does so. Anybody who loves the Son is thus loved of the Father. That is not difficult to understand from a human perspective. I find I like people who like my children. How much more must God, whose love is perfect, love those who love His Son?

Not only that, but Jesus also promises to love those who love Him, and to disclose Himself and the Father to them. That supernatural union comes with loving Jesus Christ, a personal love relationship between the believer and Christ—not religion that simply cranks out the motions, goes to church, and walks through some kind of ritual— but an honest, deep, heartfelt, committed kind of love that obeys. To that kind of love comes the manifestation of God in all His fullness, which results in the genuine supernatural union Jesus promised.

I am sure all the disciples were dumbfounded at that point. Judas— not Iscariot, but the son of James (Luke 6:16; Acts 1:13) who is also called Lebbaeus and Thaddaeus—spoke out: "'Lord, how is it that You will manifest Yourself to us, and not to the world?'" (John 14:22). He thought Jesus meant that He would physically manifest Himself and the Father. Yet he reasoned that if they could see Jesus, everyone else should be able to as well. Furthermore, Christ was to be the Savior of the world. How could He not manifest Himself to the world?

"Jesus answered and said to him, 'If anyone loves Me, he will keep My word; and My Father will love him, and We will come to him and make Our home with him. He who does not love Me does not keep My words; and the word which you hear is not Mine but the Father's who sent Me'" (vv. 23–24). Thaddaeus might not have been very satisfied with that answer; it sounds exactly like verse 21, which sounds exactly like verse 15. They all say the same thing: "If you love Me, you will keep My commandments, and I will manifest Myself to you." We begin to get the idea that this is an important concept.

The point Christ made to Thaddaeus was that He would manifest Himself in a spiritual sense—He would reveal Himself and the Father in someone's heart, to his spiritual senses. An unsaved man or woman doesn't have spiritual perception, so the only one who can comprehend the manifestation Christ referred to is one who loves Him and shows his love by obedience.

It is not a question of perfection—if we say we are without sin, we call God a liar (1 John 1:10). Nor is the issue one of earning salvation with obedience. Salvation is a gift that comes by faith. It cannot be earned or deserved. But faith that does not produce obedience is not saving faith (see James 2:17). The issue is not sinless perfection, but the direction of the redeemed life. The Lord has fellowship only with those whose hearts welcome Him and love Him and whose love is clearly indicated by their obedience. They are the ones who are truly redeemed. The world will never discern Jesus Christ because the world will not love Him. The world will never discern the Father because the Father reveals Himself only to those who love the Son.

Jesus continues in John 14:24, "'He who does not love Me does not keep My words; and the word which you hear is not Mine but the Father's who sent Me.'" How can He manifest Himself to someone who is disobedient? People in the world don't want Christ. They don't want to obey His words. They don't love Him. And since the words Jesus spoke came from the Father, the world doesn't want Him either. He manifests Himself only to those who want Him. There's not a soul in the world who wants Jesus Christ to the point of loving obedience who doesn't receive Him. But He will not manifest Himself to an unbelieving, unwanting, unloving world.

Note that Jesus claims His words are the Father's. It is the highest claim to authority He can make. He is in essence saying, "If you reject My words, you have rejected God." His words are the Father's truth. During His earthly ministry, Christ had subjected His own thoughts, words, ideas, and attitudes to the will of the Father. Therefore while they were always in perfect harmony, nevertheless, the Son was totally yielded to the Father's will.

A SUPERNATURAL TEACHER

Jesus had spoken only the Father's words, but the disciples had always had trouble understanding. For example, "Therefore, when He had risen from the dead, His disciples remembered that He had said this to them; and they believed the Scripture and the word which Jesus had said" (John 2:22). John 12:16 says, "His disciples did not understand these things at first; but when Jesus was glorified, then they remembered that these things were written about Him and that they had done these things to Him." Later during the upper room discourse Jesus said, "'I still have many things to say to you, but you cannot bear them now'" (John 16:12). The disciples had failed to understand so much of what He had already said, that He would have to suspend His teaching.

Thus Christ was turning over the continuing instruction to the Holy Spirit, who would dwell in them. "'These things I have spoken to you while being present with you. But the Helper, the Holy Spirit, whom the Father will send in My name, He will teach you all things, and bring to your remembrance all things that I said to you'" (John 14:25–26). Now the Spirit is a resident Teacher who dwells within every believer.

The Holy Spirit comes in the name of Christ. That means, of course, that He comes in Christ's stead. Christ had come in the name of the Father. Neither the Spirit nor the Son carries on His own ministry independently. The Holy Spirit's ministry is to stand in this world in the place of Christ. He desires what Christ desires, loves what Christ loves, does what Christ would do, and thus brings glory to Christ, not to Himself.

So God gave His truth to Christ, who gave it to the Holy Spirit, who reveals it to us. The Spirit receives nothing of Himself, seeks no glory of His own, and desires only to manifest the glory of Jesus Christ.

His role is that of a Teacher: "He will teach you all things, and bring to your remembrance all things that I said to you" (v. 26). That does not mean, of course, that the Holy Spirit imparts to us some kind of omniscience. "All things" is used here in a relative sense. It means "all things pertaining to spiritual maturity."

A secondary application of this promise is that the Holy Spirit would enable the disciples to recall the words Jesus had spoken to them so that when they recorded them as Scripture, the words would be perfect and error free. It is a promise of divine inspiration.

Can you imagine their trying, with no supernatural help, to put together a record of Jesus' words? They had to have a supernatural Teacher to record accurately Jesus' words as Scripture. In addition, the Spirit would reveal new truth. Those whom God chose wrote it down, resulting in the Word of God as we have it today. To question the accuracy or the integrity of it is to deny this crucial aspect of the Spirit's role.

Faith in the inerrancy of biblical inspiration is fundamental to sound doctrine. Those who give up the inspiration of the Bible have given up the basis of Christianity. History has repeatedly borne that out. Churches, seminaries, and denominations that have yielded ground on the issue of inspiration have opened the floodgates to rationalism, compromise, and ultimately, total apostasy.

How does the promise that the Holy Spirit will instruct us and bring all things to our memory apply today? The Spirit guides us in our pursuit of truth through the Word of God. He teaches us by convicting us of sin, affirming the truth in our heart, and opening our understanding to the depths of truth God has revealed. He often brings to mind appropriate verses and truths from Scripture at just the right time.

Matthew 10:19 is a promise to the apostles as Christ sent them on a mission to preach among the cities, but it shows how the Spirit of God works, even today: "'But when they deliver you up [to be tried for your faith], do not worry about how or what you should speak. For it will be given to you in that hour what you should speak.'"

Nothing can take the place of the Holy Spirit's work in the life of the believer. Through Him we are "heirs of God and joint heirs with Christ" (Rom. 8:17), infinitely richer than all the billionaires of the world put together, because what we possess is not a passing thing—ours is an eternal inheritance.

Paul, quoting Isaiah, wrote, "Eye has not seen, nor ear heard, nor have entered into the heart of man the things which God has prepared for those who love Him" (1 Cor. 2:9). Christians are rich beyond imagination. And the greatest resource of all—the Holy Spirit—dwells in us and is with us forever.

SEVEN

THE PEACE OF CHRIST

T HE HEBREW BIBLE OFTEN USES A FAMILIAR BUT SIGNIFICANT word, *shalom*. In its purest sense, *shalom* means "peace." The connotation is positive. That is, when someone says, "Shalom," or, "Peace unto you," it doesn't mean, "I hope you don't get into any trouble"; it means, "I hope you have all the highest good coming your way."

Most people in our world don't understand peace as a positive concept. All they think of is the absence of trouble. The definition of peace in many languages of the world illustrates that. For example, the Quechua Indians in Ecuador and Bolivia use a word for peace that literally translates, "to sit down in one's heart." For them, peace is the opposite of running around in the midst of constant anxieties. The Chol Indians of Mexico define peace as "a quiet heart." Those may be beautiful ways to put it, but they still seem to leave us with only the negative idea that peace is the absence of trouble.

Close to the meaning of the Hebrew word *shalom* is the word used by the Kekchi Indians of Guatemala, who define peace as "quiet goodness." The term they use conveys the idea of something that is active and aggressive, not just a rest in one's own heart away from troublesome circumstances.

The biblical concept of peace does not focus on the absence of trouble. Biblical peace is unrelated to circumstances—it is a goodness of life that is not touched by what happens on the outside. You may be in the midst of great trials and still have biblical peace. The Apostle Paul said he could be content in any circumstance; and he demonstrated that he had peace even in the jail at Philippi, where he sang and remained confident that God was being gracious to him. Then when the opportunity arose, he communicated God's goodness to the Philippian jailer and brought him and his family to salvation. Likewise, James wrote, "My brethren, count it all joy when you fall into various trials" (James 1:2).

Where does a person find the kind of peace that is not just the absence of trouble—but is the kind of peace that cannot even be affected by trouble, danger, or sorrow? It is ironic that what is surely the most definitive discourse on peace in all of Scripture comes from the Lord Jesus on the night before He died in agony. He knew what He was facing, yet He still took time to comfort His disciples with the message of peace: "'Peace I leave with you, My peace I give to you; not as the world gives do I give to you. Let not your heart be troubled, neither let it be afraid'" (John 14:27).

The peace Jesus is speaking of enables believers to remain calm in the most wildly fearful circumstances. It enables them to hush a cry, still a riot, rejoice in pain and trial, and sing in the middle of suffering. This peace is never affected by circumstances but instead affects and even overrules them.

THE NATURE OF PEACE

The New Testament speaks of two kinds of peace—the objective peace concerning your relationship to God, and the subjective peace concerning your experience in life.

The unregenerate person lacks peace with God. That was once true of all of us. We come into the world fighting against God, because we are a part of the rebellion that started with Adam and Eve. Romans 5:10 says we were enemies of God. We fought against God, and everything we did militated against His principles.

But when we receive Jesus Christ, we cease being enemies of God—we make a truce with Him. We come over to His side, and the hostility is ended. Jesus Christ wrote the peace treaty with His blood shed at the Cross. That treaty, that bond, that covenant declares the objective fact that we now are at peace with Him.

That's what Paul means in Ephesians 6:15, when he calls the good news of salvation "the preparation of the gospel of peace." The gospel is that which makes a person who was at war with God to be at peace with Him. This peace is objective—that is, it has nothing to do with how we feel or what we think. It is an accomplished fact.

Romans 5:1 says, "Therefore, having been justified by faith, we have peace with God." We who trust Christ are redeemed and declared righteous by faith. Our sins are forgiven, rebellion ceases, the war is over, and we have peace with God. That was God's wonderful purpose in salvation.

Colossians 1:20–22 says that Christ "made peace through the blood of His cross. And you, who once were alienated and enemies in your mind by wicked works, yet now He has reconciled in the body of His flesh through death, to present you holy, and blameless, and above reproach."

A sinful, vile, wicked individual cannot come into the presence of a holy God. Something must make that unholy person righteous before he can be at peace with God. And that's exactly what Christ did when He died for sin and imputed His righteousness to all who believe. So Paul says we are no longer enemies but are at peace because we are reconciled.

It is as if God were on one side, we were on the other side, then Christ filled the gap, taking the hand of God and the hand of man and placing them together into the same grip. Jesus Christ has now brought us together with God through His work on the Cross.

Whereas God and man were once estranged, they have now been reconciled. That is the heart of the gospel message, as Paul says in 2 Corinthians 5:18–19, "Now all things are of God, who has reconciled us to Himself through Jesus Christ, and has given us the ministry of reconciliation, that is, that God was in Christ reconciling the world to Himself, not imputing their trespasses to them, and has committed to us the word of reconciliation."

But Jesus is not talking about objective peace in John 14:27. The peace He speaks of there is a subjective, experiential peace. It is tranquillity of the soul, a settled, positive peace that affects the circumstances of life. It is peace that is aggressive; rather than being victimized by events, it attacks them and gobbles them up. It is a supernatural, permanent, positive, no-side-effects, divine tranquillizer. This peace is the heart's calm after Calvary's storm. It is the firm conviction that He who spared not His own Son will also along with Him freely give us all things (Rom. 8:32).

This is the peace that Paul speaks about in Philippians 4:7: "And the peace of God, which surpasses all understanding, will guard your hearts and minds through Christ Jesus." The peace of God is not based on circumstances like the world's peace, so it doesn't always make sense to the carnal mind. Paul says it is a peace that surpasses understanding. It doesn't seem reasonable that such peace could exist in the midst of the problems and troubles Christians go through. But this is divine, supernatural peace; it cannot be figured out on a human level.

The word for "guard" in Philippians 4:7 is not the word that means to "watch" or "keep imprisoned." It is a word that is often used in a military sense, meaning "to stand at a post and guard against the aggression of an enemy." When peace is on guard, the Christian has entered an impregnable citadel from which nothing can dislodge him. The name of the fortress is Christ, and the guard is peace. The peace of God stands guard and keeps worry from corroding our hearts and unworthy thoughts from tearing up our minds.

This is the kind of peace people really want. They want a peace that deals with the past, one where no strings of conscience dipped in the poison of past sins bind at them and torture them hour by hour. They want a peace that governs the present, with no unsatisfied desires gnawing at their hearts. They want a peace that holds promise for the future, where no foreboding fear of the unknown and dark tomorrow threatens them. And that is exactly the peace through which the guilt of the past is forgiven; by which the trials of the present are overcome; and in which our destiny in the future is secured eternally.

THE SOURCE OF PEACE

This subjective, experiential peace—the peace *of* God—has its foundation in the objective, factual peace—peace *with* God. The peace *of* God is not obtainable by those who are not at peace *with* God. God alone brings peace. In fact, in Philippians 4:9, 1 Thessalonians 5:23, and again in Hebrews 13:20, He is called "the God of peace."

Jesus Christ is the One who gives God's peace: "My peace I give to you." Notice He says "*My* peace." Here is the key to the supernatural nature of this peace: it is Jesus' own personal peace. It is the same deep, rich peace that stilled His heart in the midst of mockers, haters, murderers, traitors, and everything else He faced. He had a calm about Him that was extraordinary and unlike the normal human reaction. In the midst of incomprehensible resistance and persecution, He was calm and unfaltering beyond human understanding—He was a rock.

Those who knew Him might have come to expect it, but you can imagine how it must have confounded His enemies and those who didn't know Him to see someone that calm. When Jesus appeared before Pilate, He was so calm, so serene, so controlled, and so at peace, that Pilate became greatly disturbed. He was furious that Jesus was standing before him in such fearless peace. In a near frenzy, Pilate said, "'Do You not know that I have power to crucify You, and power to release You?'" (John 19:10).

Then in perfect peace Jesus replied, "'You could have no power at all against Me unless it had been given you from above'" (v. 11). That's the kind of peace Jesus is talking about in John 14:27. That's the kind He gives to us. It is undistracted fearlessness and trust. So the source of peace is Christ.

In fact, Christ is seen throughout the New Testament as the dispenser of peace. In Acts 10:36, Peter preaches about "the word which God sent to the children of Israel, preaching peace through Jesus Christ." Second Thessalonians 3:16 says, "Now may the Lord of peace Himself give you peace always in every way." Jesus Christ gives us His own personal peace. It has been tested; it was Christ's own shield and His own helmet that served Him in spiritual battle. And He gave it to us when He left. It should give us the same serenity in danger, the same calm in trouble, and the same freedom from anxiety.

THE GIVER OF PEACE

The Holy Spirit is the One who dispenses this peace as a gift. (In Galatians 5:22, one aspect of the fruit of the Spirit is peace.) You might ask, if it was Christ's peace, why is the Holy Spirit giving it? The answer is in John 16:14, which says, "'He will glorify Me, for He will take of what is Mine and declare it to you.'" The Holy Spirit's ministry is to take the things of Christ and give them to us.

Notice that every promise Jesus made to His troubled disciples on the night before His death was rooted in the coming of the Holy Spirit. Christ promised life, union with God, full understanding, and peace to those who are His disciples, but it is the Spirit of God who takes the things of Christ and gives them to us.

THE CONTRAST OF JESUS' PEACE AND THE WORLD'S PEACE

In John 14:27, Jesus says, "'Not as the world gives do I give to you.'" In other words, His peace is not like the peace of the world. The world's peace is worthless. Since 36 B.C. there have been nearly 15,000 wars. Before World War II the world had an average of 2.61 new wars every year. But since World War II, despite all of mankind's "enlightenment" and organized efforts for world peace, there have been on the average three new wars every year. We're compelled to agree with the leading newspaper that once observed, "Peace is a fable."

The only peace this world can know is shallow and unfulfilling. Most people's pursuit of peace is only an attempt to get away from problems. That is why people seek peace through alcohol, drugs, or other forms of escapism. The fact is, apart from God, there is no real peace in this world. The peace of putting your blinders on, of going to bed and forgetting it, is fleeting and worthless. And yet people try desperately to hold on to this kind of mock peace.

It is a futile pursuit. The ungodly can never know true peace. They might know only a momentary tranquillity—a shallow feeling, perhaps stimulated by positive circumstances mixed with a lot of ignorance. In fact, if unsaved people knew what destiny awaited them without God, the illusory peace borne out of ignorance would evaporate instantly.

People today live in a form of existential shock. They don't understand who they are, where they are going, or what they are going to do when they get there—if they get there. I once saw a sign on a man's desk that said, "I've got so many troubles that if anything else happens to me, it will be two weeks before I can even worry about it."

That is a commentary on the plight of modern man; but the truth is, the real reason a person can't find peace has nothing to do with emotions or environment. If you lack peace, it is not because of your mother, your father, your grandmother, the church you were reared in, or a bad experience when you were a child. The Bible tells us why men don't know peace: "The heart is deceitful above all things, and desperately wicked" (Jer. 17:9). Isaiah 48:22 says, "'There is no peace,' says the LORD, 'for the wicked.'" Man's heart is desperately wicked, and thus he cannot find peace.

Throughout the land of Judah in Jeremiah's day, problems were rising up fast. A great army was coming in to destroy Jerusalem and take the people into captivity, and they were frightened. God's enemies were removing peace from the land, and there was destruction coming like Judah had never experienced.

Jeremiah 6:14 says, "'They have also healed the hurt of My people slightly, saying, "Peace, peace!" when there is no peace.'" In other words, they tried to patch up their evil ways and then said, "Peace, peace, everything is okay." There was a lot of talk about peace, but there was not genuine peace. In Jeremiah 8:15, the prophet declares, "'We looked for peace, but no good came; and for a time of health, and there was trouble!'"

A few chapters later, Jeremiah repeats the same observation: "Have You utterly rejected Judah? Has Your soul loathed Zion? Why have You stricken us so that there is no healing for us? We looked for peace, but there was no good; and for the time of healing, and there was trouble" (14:19). Further on, the prophet put his finger on the source of the trouble: "'Do not enter the house of mourning, nor go to lament or bemoan them; for I have taken away My peace from this people,' says the LORD" (16:5). Where there was sin, there could be no peace.

We can expect nothing different in the end times. Revelation 6:4 says that when the Tribulation begins there will be a brief period of peace, but after about three and a half years, peace will be taken from the earth. Luke 21:26 says men's hearts will fail them from fear. In other words, people will be dropping dead from heart attacks caused by fear.

The world's version of peace is false. It's a lie and can't satisfy. No man without Jesus Christ can ever have real peace, and no world without God can ever know such peace. If a person has a moment of peace in this world, it is only a camouflage hiding the eternal pressure of God's judgment.

THE RESULT OF PEACE

Jesus tells us the proper response to His promise of peace, "'Let not your heart be troubled, neither let it be afraid'" (John 14:27). We ought to be able to lay hold of this peace. It is there, it is ours; but we must first take hold of it. It is interesting that He says, "My peace I give to you," then He says, "Let not your heart be troubled." The peace He gives has to be received and applied in our lives. If we lay hold of the promise of Christ's genuine peace, we will have calm, untroubled hearts, regardless of external circumstances.

If you have a troubled heart, it is because you do not believe God—you do not really trust His promise of peace. Anxiety and turmoil seldom focus on present circumstances. Normally, anxiety is trouble borrowed from either the past or the future. Some people worry about things that might happen. Others' anxieties come out of the past. But both the future and the past are under the care of God. He promises to supply our future need, and He has forgiven the past. Don't worry about tomorrow or yesterday. Jesus teaches, "'Sufficient for the day is its own trouble'" (Matt. 6:34). Concentrate on trusting God for *today's* needs.

The peace of Christ is a great resource in helping us to know the will of God. Colossians 3:15 says, "Let the peace of God rule in your hearts, to which also you were called in one body; and be thankful." The word translated "rule" is from the Greek word *brabeuo*, which means "to umpire." Paul was urging the Colossians to so depend on the peace of Christ that it became an umpire in the decisions they had to make in life.

Do you have a problem, or a decision to make? Let the peace of Christ make that decision for you. If you have examined a planned action in the light of God's Word, and His Word does not forbid you from going ahead with it, then you can more than likely carry out your plan. If you can do it and retain the peace of Christ in your heart, you can usually have the confidence that your plan is within God's will. But if you don't have that sense of peace and God's blessing about the action, don't do it.

A potential decision may make good sense from the rational point of view. But will it rob your soul of rest and peace? Do you have a sense of confidence that God is in this? If you don't have peace, it is probably the wrong thing to do. Let Christ's peace be the umpire that makes the calls. That is how we are to govern our behavior.

There are two conspicuous reasons I don't like to sin. One is that sin is an offense to the Holy God I love. He hates sin, and my love for Him makes me want to please Him. The other reason is that I don't like the way I feel after I sin. Sin destroys my sense of peace, and it breaks my sense of communion with God.

Look again at Colossians 3:15. Paul says there that peace belongs to every Christian. He calls it "the peace of God . . . to which also you were called in one body." Our peace with God and the peace of God that rules our hearts is a foundation of Christian unity. If we disregard that peace, if we refuse to let it be the umpire, we cannot have unity in the body of Christ, for everyone will be doing his own thing, and the body will be divided.

The peace of Christ is also an unending source of strength in the midst of difficulties. As Stephen sank bleeding and bruised under the stones of a cursing mob, he offered a loving, forgiving prayer for his murderers, "Lord, do not charge them with this sin" (Acts 7:60). Paul was driven out of one city, dragged almost lifeless out of another, stripped by robbers, and arraigned before ruler after ruler. Yet he had an uncanny peace. He writes,

From the Jews five times I received forty stripes minus one. Three times I was beaten with rods; once I was stoned; three times I was shipwrecked; a night and a day I have been in the deep; in journeys often, in perils of waters, in perils of robbers, in perils of my own countrymen, in perils of the Gentiles, in perils in the city, in perils in the wilderness, in perils in the sea, in perils among false brethren; in weariness and toil, in sleeplessness often, in hunger and thirst, in fastings often, in cold and nakedness—besides the other things, what comes upon me daily: my deep concern for all the churches. Who is weak, and I am not weak? Who is made to stumble, and I do not burn with indignation? (2 Cor. 11:24–29)

That is the same kind of peace you and I have for extremely difficult circumstances; the Apostle Paul just applied what was his. He says,

We are hard pressed on every side, yet not crushed; we are perplexed, but not in despair; persecuted, but not forsaken; struck down, but not destroyed—always carrying about in the body the dying of the Lord Jesus, that the life of Jesus also may be manifested in our body. For we who live are always delivered to death for Jesus' sake, that the life of Jesus also may be manifested in our mortal flesh. (2 Cor. 4:8–11)

The apostle further states, "Therefore we do not lose heart. Even though our outward man is perishing, yet our inward man is being renewed day by day. For our light affliction, which is but for a moment, is working for us a far more exceeding and eternal weight of glory, while we do not look at the things which are seen, but at the things which are not seen. For the things which are seen are temporary, but the things which are not seen are eternal" (vv. 16–18). In other words, Paul didn't focus on his problems, but on the promises of God to sustain and ultimately glorify him. Trouble comes and goes, but glory is eternal. Paul understood that, and that's why in the midst of his trials he could write to the Philippians, "Rejoice in the Lord always. Again I will say, rejoice!" (Phil. 4:4).

To have that supernatural peace available puts us under obligation to lean on it. Colossians 3:15 is not a command to seek peace, but rather a plea to let the Lord's peace work in us: "And let the peace of God rule in your hearts." You have this peace, now let it rule.

Perfect peace comes when our focus is *off* the problem, *off* the trouble, and constantly *on* Christ. Isaiah 26:3 says, "You will keep him in perfect peace, whose mind is stayed on You, because he trusts in You."

In the midst of a society where we are constantly bombarded with advertising and other worldly pressures designed to get us to focus on our needs and problems, how can we keep our minds focused on Christ? By studying the Word of God and allowing the Holy Spirit to teach us—by permitting Him to fix our hearts on the person of Jesus Christ.

Most people who lack peace simply have not taken the time to pursue it. God's peace comes to those with the personal discipline to stop in the midst of the maelstrom of life and take time to seek Him. It is a condition of peace that we cease from life's activity and know Him. He commands, "Be still, and know that I am God" (Ps. 46:10). And to those whose minds are steadfastly fixed on Him, He gives the gift of peace.

EIGHT

WHAT JESUS' DEATH MEANT TO HIM

As we look back on the cross after almost two thousand years, we stand in awe at all that God through Jesus Christ accomplished there for us. At the Cross the very Son of God suffered shame and ridicule at the hands of wicked, murdering men. He did it willingly to provide forgiveness for our sins and access to God. God's judgment was stayed and the righteousness of Christ became ours. The Father set us free to commune with Him, and we became His children and objects of His love.

When the disciples looked forward to the Cross, they could only wonder what it meant. They had been with Jesus for three blessed years, during which He had loved them and supplied all their needs. When they heard Him talk about His death, they found it impossible to understand. How could God incarnate die, and what would life be like without their beloved Master and Teacher? Fear must have come over them at the mere thought of it; and then when they realized the time was at hand, the anticipation of loneliness set in. Looking ahead at it that awful night before He died, they could see nothing but the oppressive specter of tragedy.

The problem was the disciples' faulty perspective; they were looking at Christ's death from their own viewpoint—they gave little thought to what it meant to Him. Their faith was weak, but beyond that they had a simple problem: selfishness. They wanted Jesus to stay with them because He loved them and took care of them. In a sense they were acting like the multitudes that followed Jesus as long as He fed them, but that didn't want to pay the price of following Him wholeheartedly. They were moping around, brooding, stewing over their own dilemma, thinking only of how Jesus' death would affect their problems and their desires. Their love was superficial and based on a desire for their own good, not on a desire for the best welfare of the One they loved.

We tend to respond that same way when death touches us. We feel great sorrow, but often for the wrong reasons. We may wonder why God would take our loved one—as if we should have some guaranteed amount of time on earth together. When a Christian dies, sorrow is normal for a while, and tears can be healthy. But when it continues on for a long time, it may be because the grieving person is seeing the death only from his own perspective of personal loss instead of from the loved one's viewpoint of eternal glory (if that person was a believer). We must see a Christian's death from the right perspective—as ultimate release from the body of sin, and the start of unending joy in heaven.

Jesus' death, however, was not release from a body of sin, but rather a sinless body ravaged by bearing the sins of the world. And before He could enter into unending joy, our Lord would face a dreadful, quintessential moment of separation from the Father, accompanied by the enormous weight of a multitude of sinners' transgressions and deserved punishment.

Nevertheless, He anticipated it all with an eager heart. As the Cross drew near, He revealed to His disciples what it meant to Him:

"You have heard Me say to you, 'I am going away and coming back to you.' If you loved Me, you would rejoice because I said, 'I am going to the Father,' for My Father is greater than I. And now I have told you before it comes, that when it does come to pass, you may believe.

I will no longer talk much with you, for the ruler of this world is coming, and he has nothing in Me. But that the world may know that I love the Father, and as the Father gave Me commandment, so I do. Arise, let us go from here." (John 14:28–31)

The disciples viewed Jesus' death with sorrow, but to Him it meant joy. Had they loved Him as they should have, they would have rejoiced with Him and looked forward with Him to the four marvelous eternal works He would accomplish at the Cross. (For an extensive study of the drama and significance of Christ's death, see John MacArthur, *The Murder of Jesus* [Nashville: Word, 2000].)

GOD WOULD DIGNIFY CHRIST'S PERSON

Before the incarnation, Jesus was in eternal glory. He experienced the Father's infinite love and fellowship in a way we cannot even comprehend. But He left this glory to come to earth, not as a king to a magnificent palace, but as a tiny baby to a drab, humble stable. He lived by modest means; He had no regular place to lay His head. He suffered the hatred, abuse, and jeers of evil men. He was rejected by His own people and vilified even by the religious leaders. "He was despised and rejected by men, a Man of sorrows and acquainted with grief. And we hid, as it were, our faces from Him" (Isa. 53:3).

From our human perspective, one of the most incomprehensible truths about Jesus Christ is that He, the eternal Lord of glory, was willing to humble Himself so completely for our sakes. He stepped down from a position of equality with the Most High God and condescended to share His riches with us. Second Corinthians 8:9 says, "For you know the grace of our Lord Jesus Christ, that though He was rich, yet for your sakes He became poor, that you through His poverty might become rich." Jesus had all the riches of heaven, yet He gave them up for a while so we could later share them with Him forever.

The Book of Hebrews further explains Jesus' condescension:

> But we see Jesus, who was made a little lower than the angels, for the suffering of death crowned with glory and honor, that He, by the grace of God, might taste death for everyone. . . . Therefore, in all things He had to be made like His brethren, that He might be a merciful and faithful High Priest in things pertaining to God, to make propitiation for the sins of the people. For in that He Himself has suffered, being tempted, He is able to aid those who are tempted. (2:9, 17–18)

Jesus became one of us. He suffered what we suffer, not only so He could redeem us, but also so He could sympathize with us. The incarnation allowed Him to experience all the temptations, difficulties, griefs, and heartbreaks of people. He can empathize with us; from His own experience He understands our struggles.

Philippians 2:6–10 describes the incarnation as an act of unselfish humility by Jesus, "who, being in the form of God, did not consider it robbery to be equal with God" (v. 6). He was always equal to God, but did not covet the outward appearance of equality during His incarnation. Instead, He "made Himself of no reputation, taking the form of a bondservant, and coming in the likeness of men. And being found in appearance as a man, He humbled Himself and became obedient to the point of death, even the death of the cross" (vv. 7–8). He was willing to come down to earth and become a servant, even if that meant death on a cross.

Because the Son humbly obeyed, the Father exalted Him. Paul continues, "Therefore God also has highly exalted Him and given Him the name which is above every name, that at the name of Jesus every knee should bow, of those in heaven, and of those on earth, and of those under the earth" (vv. 9–10).

There have always been those who get confused about the humiliation of Christ. They think that because He humbled Himself and became a servant, they are not to worship Him as God. Actually, the opposite is true. Because He humbled Himself, He is to be exalted—every knee is to bow before Him and confess that Jesus Christ is Lord.

Jehovah's Witnesses, Unitarians, and others who deny the deity of Christ have misinterpreted John 14:28 by saying that Jesus is inferior to the Father. When He said, "My Father is greater than I," He referred not to His essential being, but to His role as a humbled servant. While He was humbled, the Father was in glory and therefore greater; Jesus had put Himself beneath the Father's glory.

He had also put His will beneath the Father's will. In the Garden of Gethsemane, He prayed to the Father, "'Take this cup away from Me; nevertheless, not what I will, but what You will'" (Mark 14:36).

Jesus repeatedly claimed to be equal in deity to the Father. We have already seen one example in John 14:9, when Philip asked to be shown the Father. Jesus answered, "'He who has seen Me has seen the Father.'" Jesus took on a role that was beneath the Father, but He was not inferior in nature or essence (cf. Titus 2:13).

At the end of His earthly ministry, as He approached the Cross, knowing what lay ahead of Him, Christ knelt prior to entering the Garden of Gethsemane and prayed to the Father: "'I have glorified You on the earth. I have finished the work which You have given Me to do. And now, O Father, glorify Me together with Yourself, with the glory which I had with You before the world was'" (John 17:4–5). Jesus was looking ahead to the full expression of His glory—that same pristine glory He knew before the humiliation of the incarnation.

Our Savior found joy as He approached the Cross because through His suffering there He would be restored to the full expression of deity. He looked forward to it and wanted His beloved friends to share His joy. 'If you loved Me,' He told them, 'you would rejoice because I said, "I am going to the Father," for My Father is greater than I'" (John 14:28).

Hebrews 12:2 says, "[Jesus] for the joy that was set before Him endured the cross, despising the shame, and has sat down at the right hand of the throne of God." He rejoiced because He knew the result of the Cross would be His glorification and His presence at the Father's right hand.

Some people think Jesus didn't know He was going to be crucified. He knew. He was familiar with the prophecies of Isaiah 53 and Psalm 22, both of which contain detailed accounts of the crucifixion. Obviously, even though they were written long before Christ's birth, He knew them. The crucifixion was not an afterthought, but a crucial element in the plan of God from the beginning. Our Lord knew exactly what was going to happen, but He went to the cross anyway. It was a bitter cup, but He was willing to drink it.

CHRIST WOULD DOCUMENT THE TRUTH

Jesus had made many claims about Himself to the disciples. Although they wanted to believe those claims—and for the most part they did—yet doubt would often creep into their hearts. They found much of Jesus' teaching about who He was and why He came difficult to fathom, so they teetered between belief and unbelief.

Jesus used a simple method to strengthen their faith—He would predict events. When what He said happened, the disciples would remember what He had predicted. One prophecy after another came true, and each fulfillment grounded their faith a little more. By the day of Pentecost, their faith was so strong that they fearlessly proclaimed the gospel to thousands of pilgrims gathered in Jerusalem for the festival.

Jesus acknowledged this use of prediction to strengthen their faith: "'I have told you before it comes, that when it does come to pass, you may believe'" (John 14:29). He knew the eleven didn't believe everything then, but they would when His words came true. Fulfilled prophecy is perhaps the greatest proof that our Lord's words are true.

In John 13:19 Jesus had used prediction to strengthen the disciples' faith. And there is a deep significance in His words at the end of that verse, "that . . . you may believe that I am He." The English translators added the "He" at the end of the verse. What Jesus actually said was, "I am telling you before, so that you'll believe that I am." "I AM" is God's name (Exod. 3:14). It was the same as saying, "I want you to believe that I am God." He was urging them to embrace the truth of His deity.

He had just told the disciples, among other things, that Judas Iscariot was going to betray Him. You can imagine what they thought later when they saw Judas betray Jesus in the garden. Their minds must have flashed back to what He had said earlier in the upper room. The prediction of the betrayal by Judas was just the first in a series of prophecies by Jesus that ended with the promise of a divine Helper. The disciples' faith was completely solidified by the time that last prediction was fulfilled on the day of Pentecost.

The final promise to send a divine Helper was linked with a promise of supernatural peace. On the day of Pentecost, a supernatural peace like nothing the apostles had ever known flooded their hearts as the Spirit of God took residence within them. Later, when Peter and John preached, the religious authorities confronted them and ordered them to stop. They calmly responded, "Whether it is right in the sight of God to listen to you more than to God, you judge. For we cannot but speak the things which we have seen and heard" (Acts 4:19–20).

One by one, every prophecy Jesus gave the disciples came to pass. With each one, their faith was strengthened so that they trusted Him more and more. The fulfilled prophecies fully documented the truth that He was God.

You may wonder why, if Jesus wanted to strengthen His men, He didn't simply stay on earth and continue teaching them. The reason is that He had said all He could say. Now it was time to depart and allow other prophecies to come true, to fulfill God's purpose in redemption, and to strengthen their faith as they watched it all unfold.

The events that followed did indeed strengthen the disciples' faith. Christ had said He would die on a cross, and He did. He had said He would rise, and He did. He had said He would ascend to the Father, and they saw Him ascend. He had said the Spirit would come, and it happened. He had said He would supply supernatural life, and they got it. He had promised them a supernatural union with the living God, and they experienced it. He had promised them an indwelling Teacher, and they received the Spirit of God. He had promised them peace, and they were flooded with peace. Every detail of each prophecy came to pass just as He had said. Through those events, the disciples' faith became rock solid. His words were thus documented and their faith cemented.

The Lord's leaving was really an act of love toward the disciples. He knew their faith would have to be strong if they were to carry His message to the world. They would have to move into the full blast of Satan's fire, into the furnace of hell's opposition. Seeing all His prophecies fulfilled one after another was the best way their faith could remain strong enough for that mission.

In fact, Jesus said that if they really loved Him—if they really wanted the world to hear the gospel—they would rejoice that He was leaving. In effect He was saying, "Stop looking at My death from your own perspective and look at it from My perspective. When I go, your faith will be strengthened because the truth will be fully documented in your lives; then you will take My message into all the world. But the longer I stay, the longer that proclamation will be postponed."

CHRIST WOULD DEFEAT HIS ARCHENEMY

When Jesus came to earth, His central purpose was to redeem all who place their trust in Him. The Fall had ruined humanity's fellowship with God. Following that tragedy, people were spiritually isolated and lost; they had neither communion with Him nor knowledge of Him. Christ had determined even before the foundation of the world that He would come to earth to bring fallen sinners back to God (cf. Rev. 13:8).

In order to succeed, the Lord had to defeat Satan decisively. In

John 14:30, He talks about His foe. "'I will no longer talk much with you, for the ruler of this world is coming, and he has nothing in Me.'" He calls the devil "the ruler of this world," because this world is Satan's domain, and the system of evil under which this world is oppressed is of Satan's devising.

Satan was already indwelling Judas, pushing him into the garden, where he would betray Jesus. Jesus knew that Satan was coming in the person of Judas to take Him. He knew He was about to enter the dreaded death-battle with His enemy.

Jesus had battled Satan all through His earthly life. Satan had tried to kill Him as an infant—he had caused all the male babies to be slain throughout the region where Jesus was born (Matt. 2:16). Although the Bible is largely silent regarding the first thirty years of Jesus' life, He undoubtedly faced satanic opposition at every turn. Then when He began His ministry, Satan immediately took Him out to the wilderness to tempt Him. He tried to get Jesus to bow and worship him. During Jesus' ministry, Satan tried everything. He confronted Him with people who hated Him and tried to kill Him, and with demons who tried to stop His work.

From the night of His birth to the night of His death, Satan fought against Christ. Finally, His death would resolve the age-old conflict that had raged since Lucifer's fall from heaven (cf. Isa. 14 and Ezek. 28). The outcome would be decided at Calvary. Jesus was about to win the ultimate victory.

He had always looked forward to victory over Satan. Earlier, Jesus had declared, "'Now is the judgment of this world; now the ruler of this world will be cast out. And I, if I am lifted up from the earth, will draw all peoples to Myself.'" The Apostle John adds an editorial note to those words: "This He said, signifying by what death He would die" (John 12:31–33). In other words, our Lord was saying that the ultimate defeat of Satan would be accomplished when He was "lifted up" on the cross. He went to the Cross knowing it was the final blow that would wipe out Satan's power.

While Jesus was in the garden, the soldiers arrived. He asked them, "'Have you come out, as against a robber, with swords and clubs? . . . But this is your hour, and the power of darkness'" (Luke 22:52–53). The power of darkness is Satan. He was saying, "This is the hour for My judgment on you and the power of darkness." He regarded the time on the cross as a conflict with Satan. Satan would bruise Jesus on the heel, but Jesus would crush Satan's head (cf. Gen. 3:15).

Christ became incarnate with the express purpose of destroying the devil. Hebrews 2:14 says, "Inasmuch then as the children have partaken of flesh and blood, He Himself likewise shared in the same, that through death He might destroy him who had the power of death, that is, the devil." First John 3:8 says why Jesus came: "For this purpose the Son of God was manifested, that He might destroy the works of the devil." Jesus looked at the Cross as a conflict with the devil, and He knew He would be victorious.

Since the Cross, the power of Satan has been broken. He is still active, but Christ's death and resurrection have effectively weakened him. Because he has already had his main strength broken, the devil has no power in your life unless you yield to him. Now he is the prisoner of Christ and one day will be cast into the lake of fire.

So in effect Jesus was saying to His disciples, "Look at the Cross from My perspective. I am through with this endless conflict against Satan; I've had enough of his opposition. When I go to the Cross, I'm going to destroy the devil. You shouldn't grieve, but be joyful. I'm going to defeat the archenemy, who has troubled us for ages." It turned out that all of Satan's schemes to get Jesus to the cross were only part of God's plan to destroy His enemy.

Satan tried desperately but in vain to find a place where Jesus was vulnerable. Jesus says in John 14:30, "The ruler of this world . . . has nothing in Me." Satan had looked for some sinful weakness in Him, but he couldn't find one because Jesus had none.

If Satan had been able to find any sin in Christ, our Lord would have been worthy of death. As Romans 6:23 says, "The wages of sin is death." But Hebrews 4:15 says we have a High Priest who "was in all points tempted as we are, yet without sin." As the writer of Hebrews says later in his letter, "For such a High Priest was fitting for us, who is holy, harmless, undefiled, separate from sinners, and has become higher than the heavens" (7:26). He did not sin; He could not sin. Satan had entered into conflict with One who was not vulnerable. And it was Satan who would be destroyed.

CHRIST WOULD DEMONSTRATE HIS LOVE

If Jesus did nothing to deserve death, we are left wondering why He was allowed to die. The answer is that Jesus wanted to demonstrate His love for the Father. He was voluntarily going to the Cross so "that the world may know that I love the Father, and as the Father gave Me commandment, so I do" (John 14:31). He portrayed Himself as a Son who was obedient to His Father. While it is also true that He died because He loved us, here He emphasizes His love for *the Father*. It was a supreme act of love to allow Satan to kill Him without legitimate reason, just because it was the Father's will that He die. Through His obedience, He showed the world how He loved the Father.

It is interesting that although Jesus often spoke of His *obedience* to the Father, this is the only time in the New Testament He specifically affirms His *love* for the Father. Yet each mention of His obedience implies His love.

The religious leaders of His day all claimed to love God. But theirs was a superficial imitation of love because it couldn't pass the test of obedience. Jesus had already said three times that the test of love is obedience (John 14:15, 21, 23). Now He was going to give the disciples living proof of His love; He would die because that was the Father's plan. He would die because He loved the Father—not because He deserved such a death, but because God had designed it. He wanted to show the world His love for the Father, and He rejoiced at the opportunity, for love is shown best in selfless, sacrificial service for the one loved.

You would think that as His disciples listened and learned what Jesus' death meant to Him, they would surely be jolted out of their selfish stupor. They had a difficult few days ahead, and their pain might have been greatly eased if they could only begin to see through Jesus' eyes. He wanted them to understand the grandeur of the scheme of salvation that was unfolding all around them. If only they had listened, they might have been able to perceive beyond their little, selfish sense of sorrow and loneliness. But that didn't happen until after the resurrection.

We tend to be like the disciples—concerned about our own problems and needs. Many times our prayers are full of asking but void of thanks. We beg but don't praise. Instead of looking at things selfishly—how they affect us—we should look at the way things affect the cause of Christ. We must pray that God will cure us of ourselves so we can be totally obedient to Him.

NINE

THE VINE AND THE BRANCHES

A T KEY POINTS IN HIS MINISTRY, CHRIST EMPHASIZED HIS
equality with God in the clearest possible terminology. The
strongest affirmations of His deity employed the same name God used
when He first revealed Himself to Moses—"I AM" (Exod. 3:14).

Prior to the upper room discourse, Jesus had already taught the
disciples, "'I am the bread of life'" (John 6:35), "'I am the light of
the world'" (8:12), and "'I am the door'" (10:9). The night before
His death, He told them first, "'I am the way'" (14:6), and now "'I
am the true vine'" (15:1). Like the other great "I am" passages recorded
in the Gospel of John, this figure of speech points to His deity. Each
one is a metaphor that elevates Christ to the level of Creator,
Sustainer, Savior, or Lord—titles that can be claimed only by God.

"I am the true vine, and My Father is the vinedresser. Every branch in
Me that does not bear fruit He takes away; and every branch that
bears fruit He prunes, that it may bear more fruit. You are already
clean because of the word which I have spoken to you. Abide in Me,
and I in you. As the branch cannot bear fruit of itself, unless it abides
in the vine, neither can you, unless you abide in Me. I am the vine,
you are the branches. He who abides in Me, and I in him, bears much

fruit; for without Me you can do nothing. If anyone does not abide in Me, he is cast out as a branch and is withered; and they gather them and throw them into the fire, and they are burned." (John 15:1–6)

The metaphor in this passage is of a vine and its branches. The vine is the source and sustenance of life for the branches, and the branches must abide in the vine to live and bear fruit. Jesus, of course, is the Vine, and the branches are people. While it is obvious the fruit-bearing branches represent true Christians, the identity of the fruitless ones is in question. Some commentators say the barren branches are Christians who bear no spiritual fruit. Others believe they are un-believers. As always, however, we must look to the context for the best answer.

The true meaning of the metaphor becomes clear when we con-sider the characters in that night's drama. The disciples were with Jesus. He had loved them to the uttermost; He had comforted them with the words recorded in John 14. The Father was foremost in His thoughts, because He was thinking of the events surrounding His death, which would occur the next day. But He was also aware of someone else—the betrayer. Jesus had dismissed Judas Iscariot from the fellowship when he rejected Jesus' final appeal of love.

All the characters of the drama were thus in the mind of Jesus. He saw the eleven, whom He loved deeply and passionately. He was aware of the Father, with whom He shared an infinite love. And He must have grieved over Judas, whom He had loved unconditionally.

All those characters played a part in Jesus' metaphor. The Vine is Christ; the Vinedresser is the Father. The fruit-bearing branches rep-resent the eleven and all true disciples of the church age. The fruitless branches represent Judas and all those who never were true disciples.

Jesus had long been aware of the difference between Judas and the eleven. After washing the disciples' feet, He said, "'He who is bathed needs only to wash his feet, but is completely clean; and you are clean, but not all of you.' For He knew who would betray Him;

therefore He said, 'You are not all clean'" (John 13:10–11). Once God forgives a person, he is clean and does not need the bathing of forgiveness again. That man or woman simply needs to clean the dust and dirt of daily sins from his or her feet.

Christ's point is that a child of God who commits a sin doesn't need to be saved again; he needs only to restore his personal relationship with the Father. But Judas had not even been "bathed" because he was not a child of God—and Jesus knew it. That's why He added, "You are not all clean."

As we saw in chapter 2 of our study, Judas appeared to be like the other disciples. He was with Jesus for the same amount of time—he even had the responsibility of keeping the money. It appeared he was a branch in the Vine, just as the other disciples were—but he never bore real spiritual fruit. God finally removed Judas' branch from the vine, and it was burned.

Some would say Judas had lost his salvation. According to them, the same could happen to any believer who does not bear fruit. But Jesus made a promise to His children, "'I give them eternal life, and they shall never perish; neither shall anyone snatch them out of My hand'" (John 10:28). And previously He had guaranteed the absolute security of the true child of God: "'All that the Father gives Me will come to Me, and the one who comes to Me I will by no means cast out'" (John 6:37). A genuine believer cannot lose his salvation and be condemned to hell.

A branch that is truly connected to the Vine is secure and will never be removed. But one that only appears to be connected—one that has only a superficial attachment—will be removed. If it does not have the life of the Vine flowing through it, it will not bear fruit. Those are the Judas-branches.

There are people who, like Judas, appear by human perception to be united with Christ, but they are apostates doomed to hell. They may attend church, know all the right answers, and go through religious motions; but God will remove them, and they will be burned. Others, like the eleven, are genuinely connected to the Vine and bear genuine fruit.

CHRIST IS THE TRUE VINE

Jesus was not introducing a new idea by using the metaphor of a vine and its branches. In the Old Testament, God's vine was the people of Israel. He used them to accomplish His purpose in the world, and He blessed those connected with them. He was the vinedresser; He cared for the vine, trimmed it, and cut off branches that did not bear fruit.

But God's vine degenerated and bore no fruit. The Vinedresser grieved over the tragedy of Israel's fruitlessness:

> Now let me sing to my Well-beloved a song of my Beloved regarding His vineyard: My Well-beloved has a vineyard on a very fruitful hill. He dug it up and cleared out its stones, and planted it with the choicest vine. He built a tower in its midst, and also made a winepress in it; so He expected it to bring forth good grapes, but it brought forth wild grapes. "And now, O inhabitants of Jerusalem and men of Judah, judge, please, between Me and My vineyard. What more could have been done to My vineyard that I have not done in it? Why then, when I expected it to bring forth good grapes, did it bring forth wild grapes? And now, please let Me tell you what I will do to My vineyard: I will take away its hedge, and it shall be burned; and break down its wall, and it shall be trampled down. I will lay it waste; it shall not be pruned or dug, but there shall come up briers and thorns. I will also command the clouds that they rain no rain on it." For the vineyard of the LORD of hosts is the house of Israel, and the men of Judah are His pleasant plant. He looked for justice, but behold, oppression; for righteousness, but behold, a cry for help. (Isa. 5:1–7)

God had done everything to create a fruit-producing environment, yet Israel bore none. So He took away its wall and left it unprotected.

Foreign nations then trampled down the nation and laid it waste. Israel was no longer God's vine; it had forfeited its privilege.

Now there is a new vine. No longer does blessing come through a covenantal relationship with Israel. Fruit and blessing come through a spiritual connection with Jesus Christ.

Jesus is the true vine. In Scripture, the word *true* is often used to describe what is eternal, heavenly, and divine. Israel was imperfect, but Christ is perfect; Israel was the type, but Christ is the reality.

He is also the true tabernacle, as opposed to the original, earthly tabernacle (cf. Heb. 8:2). He is the true light (John 1:9). God revealed His light before, but Christ is the perfect light; He is all that can be revealed. He is also the true bread (John 6:32). God had sustained men by manna from heaven, but Christ is the highest quality of bread, the perfect sustenance.

Jesus chose the figure of a vine for several reasons. The lowliness of a vine demonstrates His humility. The figure also pictures a close, permanent, vital union between Christ and His followers. It is symbolic of belonging, because branches belong entirely to the vine; if branches are to live and bear fruit, they must completely depend on the vine for nourishment, support, strength, and vitality.

Yet many who call themselves Christians fail to depend on Christ. Instead of being attached to the true vine, they are tied to a bank account. Others are attached to their education. Some have tried to make vines out of popularity, fame, personal skills, possessions, relationships, or fleshly desires. Some think the earthly church is their vine, and they try to attach themselves to a religious system. But none of those things can sustain people for eternity and produce spiritual fruit. The vine is Christ.

THE FATHER IS THE VINEDRESSER

In the metaphor, Christ is a plant, but the Father is a person. Certain false teachers have claimed that it therefore shows Christ is not divine, but lower in character and essence than the Father. They say if He is God, His and the Father's parts in the metaphor should be equal; He should be the vine, and the Father should be the root of the vine.

But to make such a claim is to miss the whole point of Jesus' metaphor and the reason the Apostle John included it in his gospel. While He is affirming His equality in essence with the Father—by claiming to be the source and sustainer of life—Jesus is also emphasizing the fundamental difference between His role and the Father's. The point is that the Father cares for the Son and for those joined to the Son by faith.

The disciples were familiar with the role of the vinedresser. After a vine is planted, the vinedresser has two duties. First, he cuts off fruitless branches, which take away sap from the fruit-bearing branches. If sap is wasted, the plant will bear less fruit. Then, he constantly trims shoots from the fruit bearing branches so that all the sap is concentrated on fruit-bearing. Jesus applies those activities to the spiritual realm: "'Every branch in Me that does not bear fruit He takes away; and every branch that bears fruit He prunes, that it may bear more fruit'" (John 15:2).

The fruitless branches that are cut off are useless. Since they do not burn well, they cannot even be used to warm a house. They are thrown into piles and burned like garbage. As verse 2 says, God "takes away" such branches. He doesn't repair them; He removes them.

Those who are removed only appear to be connected to Christ. They don't really abide in the Vine. Like Judas, they were never really saved. At some point, the Father removes them to preserve the life and fruitfulness of the other branches.

The Father prunes the fruit-bearing branches so they will bear more fruit. We know these branches represent Christians, because only Christians can bear fruit. Pruning is not done only once—it is a constant process. After continual pruning, a branch bears much fruit. "'By this My Father is glorified, that you bear much fruit'" (John 15:8).

THE FATHER REMOVES THE FRUITLESS BRANCHES

Fruit-bearing and non-fruit-bearing branches grow rapidly, and the vinedresser must carefully prune both. If there is to be a large quantity of fruit, he must remove the fruitless branches as well as the shoots that grow on the fruit-bearing branches.

In first-century Palestine, it was common to prevent a vine from bearing fruit for three years after it was planted. In the fourth year it was strong enough to bear fruit. The careful pruning had increased its fruit-bearing capacity. Mature branches, which had already been through the four-year process, were pruned annually between December and January.

Jesus said His followers were like mature branches that bore fruit but needed pruning. There is no such thing as a fruitless Christian. Every Christian bears some fruit. You may have to look hard to find even a small grape, but if you look diligently enough, you will find something.

It is the essence of the Christian life to bear fruit. Ephesians 2:10 says, "For we are His workmanship, created in Christ Jesus for good works, which God prepared beforehand that we should walk in them." The fruit of salvation is good works. James 2:17 explains the close relationship between faith and works: "Thus also faith by itself, if it does not have works, is dead." If saving faith is legitimate, it produces fruit. That does not mean works save a person, but works are evidence that his or her faith is genuine.

Jesus said a genuine believer can be tested by his fruit. "'You will know them by their fruits. Do men gather grapes from thornbushes or figs from thistles? Even so, every good tree bears good fruit, but a bad tree bears bad fruit'" (Matt. 7:16–17). Jesus' illustration would make no sense if every Christian does not bear at least some fruit.

John the Baptist recognized the connection between salvation and fruit bearing. When he saw the Pharisees and Sadducees coming to be baptized, he said, "'Brood of vipers! Who warned you to flee from

the wrath to come? Therefore bear fruits worthy of repentance'"
(Matt. 3:7–8). Lack of fruit showed that their repentance was not
genuine.

Since all Christians bear fruit, it is clear that the fruitless branches
in John 15 cannot refer to them. In fact, the fruitless branches had to
be eliminated and thrown into the fire. Yet, in verse 2, Jesus refers to
the fruitless branches as those who are "in Me." If they are "in Him,"
are they not genuine believers?

Not necessarily. Other passages in Scripture show it is possible to
be attached to the vine without being a true believer. For example,
Romans 9:6 says, "For they are not all Israel who are of Israel." A person can be part of the nation of Israel yet not be a true Israelite.
Likewise, one can be a branch without abiding in the true Vine. In a
similar metaphor, Romans 11:17–24 represents Israel as an olive tree
from which God has removed branches. Those branches were cut off
because of unbelief (v. 20).

Some only appear to be a part of God's people. Luke 8:18 says,
"Therefore take heed how you hear. For whoever has, to him more
will be given; and whoever does not have, even what he seems to have
will be taken from him." Those who only appear to belong God will
ultimately remove from association with His family.

Clearly, some who appear to be in Christ do not truly abide in
Him. First John 2:19 explains it well: "They went out from us, but
they were not of us; for if they had been of us, they would have continued with us; but they went out that they might be made manifest,
that none of them were of us."

If you are religious, you need to be sure your relationship to
Christ is genuine. The Apostle Paul admonishes, "Examine yourselves
as to whether you are in the faith. Test yourselves. Do you not know
yourselves, that Jesus Christ is in you?—unless indeed you are dis-
qualified" (2 Cor. 13:5). We thus have a stern warning from Scripture
to check our own lives and make sure our salvation is real. This is serious; a branch that does not bear fruit is taken away and burned.

Those who say the discarded branches are Christians have a problem: the branches are burned. If those branches are Christians, it would mean they have lost their salvation forever.

But those fruitless branches are Judas-branches, false branches, people who associate themselves with Jesus and His Body and put on a facade of faith in Him. But even though such people may appear to be connected to Christ, their association is superficial. So the Father removes them.

THE FATHER PRUNES THE FRUITFUL BRANCHES

Although the fruitless branches are removed from the Vine and burned, the Father tenderly cares for the fruit-bearing branches. Jesus told His disciples, "'Every branch that bears fruit He prunes, that it may bear more fruit'" (John 15:2). The Vinedresser prunes *all* the fruit-bearing branches so they will bear much fruit.

Kathairo is the original Greek word for "prune" or "cleanse." In farming, it referred to cleaning the husks off grain and cleaning the soil before planting crops. In the metaphor of the vine, it refers to cleaning shoots off branches.

In first-century Palestine, vinedressers removed shoots in several ways. Sometimes the tip was pinched off so the shoot would grow more slowly. Larger branches were topped to prevent them from becoming too long and weak. Unwanted flower or grape clusters were thinned out.

Pruning is also necessary in our spiritual lives. The Father removes sins and the superfluous things that limit our fruitfulness. One of the best ways to cleanse us is to allow suffering and problems to come into our lives—God prunes us with a vinedresser's knife. Sometimes it hurts, and we wonder if He knows what He's doing. It may seem you are the only branch getting pruned while other branches need it more. But the Vinedresser knows what He is doing.

Sufferings and trials can take many forms: sickness, hardships, loss of material possessions, persecution or slander from unbelievers. For some, it is the loss of a loved one or grief in a relationship. There may be a combination of difficulties. Whatever the method, spiritual pruning narrows our focus and strengthens the quality of our fruit.

During any time of pruning, we can be assured God cares about us and wants us to bear much fruit. He wants to free us from the shoots that drain our life and energy. He continues His care throughout our lives to keep us spiritually healthy and productive.

Knowing the Father's love and concern should change the way we look at trials. He does not allow us to experience problems and struggles for no purpose. The problems He permits are designed to develop us so we can bear more fruit. "For whom the LORD loves He chastens, and scourges every son whom He receives" (Heb. 12:6).

Do you look at trials and problems as pruning done by our loving Vinedresser? Or do you lapse into self-pity, fear, complaining, and brooding? Perhaps you feel God has good intentions but just doesn't know what He's doing. Or maybe you ask, "God, why me? Why do I have to have problems when it seems like no one else does?"

If we remember that God is trying to make us more fruitful, we can look past the pruning process to the goal. It is thrilling to realize that God wants our lives to bear much fruit. The writer of Hebrews further encourages us to have a proper perspective on God's perfecting process: "If you endure chastening, God deals with you as with sons; for what son is there whom a father does not chasten?" (12:7).

Pruning can be painful, but the fruit—holiness—is well worth the process.

"For they [our earthly fathers] indeed for a few days chastened us as seemed best to them, but He for our profit, that we may be partakers of His holiness" (v. 10).

The Vinedresser's pruning knife is the Word of God. Jesus told the disciples, "'You are already clean because of the word which I have spoken to you'" (John 15:3). The word here translated "clean" is the same word He used in verse 2 to describe the pruning process. God's Word cleans the sin out of our lives and stimulates fruitfulness.

The Father uses affliction to make us more responsive to His Word. Most of us become more sensitive to the truth of Scripture when we are in trouble. When we have a particular problem, a verse of Scripture sometimes will seem to jump off the page. In adversity, the Word of God comes alive.

Charles Spurgeon once said, "The Word is often the knife with which the great Husbandman prunes the vine; and, brothers and sisters, if we were more willing to feel the edge of the Word, and to let it cut away something that may be very dear to us, we should not need so much pruning by affliction. It is because that first knife does not always produce the desired result that another sharp tool is used by which we are effectually pruned." (*Spurgeon's Expository Encyclopedia,* vol. 4 [Grand Rapids: Baker Books, 1977 reprint], 337)

The pruning process definitely helps us bear more fruit. If there is no fruit in your life—if there is no genuine connection to Jesus Christ—you are in danger of being removed and cast into the fire of hell. If there is fruit in your life, you can rejoice when God uses the pruning knife of affliction to make you more effective, and you can be glad the Vinedresser's ultimate goal is that you bear much fruit.

TEN

THE BENEFITS OF LIFE IN CHRIST

OUR RELATIONSHIP TO JESUS CHRIST IS UNLIKE ANYTHING ELSE in the human realm. We can describe it only by comparing it to earthly relationships we are familiar with. It is like a deep friendship. It is like two people in love with each other, or like the love and respect shared by a father and child.

Scripture uses a number of metaphors to describe our relationship to Christ. He is the King and we are the subjects; He is the Shepherd and we are the sheep; He is the Head and we are the body. One of the best metaphors is the one Christ Himself used in John 15, where He is the Vine and we are the branches.

As we saw in the previous chapter of our study, the vine-and-branches concept makes an ideal metaphor of the Christian life because it is filled with parallels to our relationship with Christ. A branch grows through its connection with the vine, and we grow because of our relationship with Christ. A branch is nothing apart from the vine, and we can do nothing apart from Him. A branch draws strength from the vine, and we become strong through Him.

In the metaphor of John 15, Christ is the Vine and the Father is the Vinedresser. The Father prunes the fruit bearing branches to make them bear more fruit. He removes the fruitless branches, and they are burned. Through continual pruning, the fruitfulness of the vine is increased. The branches that abide in the Vine—those who are truly in Christ—are blessed; they grow and bear fruit, and the Father lovingly tends them. As Jesus continues His teaching in John 15:7–11, He paints a beautiful picture of the Christian life and helps us understand and appreciate the blessings associated with abiding in Christ:

> "If you abide in Me, and My words abide in you, you will ask what you desire, and it shall be done for you. By this My Father is glorified, that you bear much fruit; so you will be My disciples.
>
> "As the Father loved Me, I also have loved you; abide in My love. If you keep My commandments, you will abide in My love, just as I have kept My Father's commandments and abide in His love.
>
> "These things I have spoken to you, that My joy may remain in you, and that your joy may be full."

FRUITFULNESS

Before examining the promised blessings in verses 7–11, we need to be completely clear regarding the true nature of biblical fruit bearing and the scriptural definition of fruitfulness. Jesus just told the disciples, "'Abide in Me, and I in you. As the branch cannot bear fruit of itself, unless it abides in the vine, neither can you, unless you abide in Me'" (v. 4). The person who abides discovers that his soul is nourished with the truths of God as he stays in a close, living, energized relationship with Jesus Christ. The natural result of that is spiritual fruit. Those who truly abide will bear fruit.

Sometimes we think we can bear fruit alone. We become independent because we think we are strong or clever. Or sometimes we look at fruit we have borne in the past and think we can produce new fruit in our own strength. We forget God worked through us to produce the fruit.

In nature, a branch can bear no fruit apart from its vine. Even strong branches can't bear fruit independently of the vine. The strongest branches, cut off from the vine, become as helpless as the weakest; the most beautiful are as helpless as the ugliest, and the best are as worthless as the worst.

Similarly, spiritual fruit bearing is not a matter of being strong or weak, good or bad, brave or cowardly, clever or foolish, experienced or inexperienced. Whatever your gifts, accomplishments, or virtues, they cannot produce fruit if you are detached from Jesus Christ.

Christians who think they are bearing fruit even though they are not closely attached to the Vine are only tying on artificial fruit. They run around straining to produce fruit but accomplish nothing. We bear fruit not by trying, but by abiding.

To bear genuine fruit, you must get as close to the True Vine, our Lord Jesus Christ, as you can. Strip away all the things of the world. Put aside the sins that distract you and sap your energy. Put aside everything that robs you of a deep, personal, loving relationship with Jesus. Stay apart from sin and be in God's Word.

Having done all that, don't worry about bearing fruit. It is not your concern. The Vine will merely use you to bear fruit. Get close to Jesus Christ, and His energy in you will bear fruit.

At times, some Christians find reading the Bible insipid and boring; they think sharing their faith is dull. Others find those things exciting. Invariably, the difference is that one is focusing on the deeds, and the other is concentrating on his relationship with Jesus Christ. Don't focus on the deeds; focus on your walk with Christ, and the righteous deeds will grow naturally out of your relationship.

Fruit is a frequent metaphor in Scripture. The main word for it is used approximately a hundred times in the Old Testament and seventy times in the New Testament; it appears in twenty-four of the twenty-seven New Testament books. It is mentioned often, yet it is also often misunderstood.

Fruit is not outward success. Many think that if a ministry is big and involves a lot of people, it is fruitful. But a church or Bible study group isn't successful just because it has many people—human effort can produce big numbers. Some missionaries minister to just a few people, but those servants of Christ bear much fruit.

Fruit bearing is not dependent on one's winsome personality. A person does not have a lot of fruit because he is enthusiastic or can make others enthusiastic about a church program. God produces real fruit in our lives when we abide.

The fruit of the Spirit is common to all believers, yet the Spirit uses each person differently. Fruit cannot be produced by simulating the genuine fruit another person has borne. It is often tempting to see the fruit another person has produced and try to duplicate it. Instead of abiding, we try to produce what someone else has produced, but we end up with only artificial fruit. God did not design us to produce the same kind of fruit. Our fruit is uniquely arranged, ordered, and designed.

Real fruit is, first of all, *Christlike character.* A believer whose character is like Christ's bears fruit. That is what the Apostle Paul means in Galatians 5:22–23, "But the fruit of the Spirit is love, joy, peace, long-suffering, kindness, goodness, faithfulness, gentleness, self-control. Against such there is no law." Those were all traits of our Lord Jesus.

Christlike character is not produced by self-effort. It grows naturally out of a relationship with Christ. We don't first try to be loving, and when we have become loving, try to be joyful, and so on. Instead, those qualities become part of our lives as we abide in Christ.

Second, *thankful praise to God* is fruit. Hebrews 13:15 says, "Therefore by Him let us continually offer the sacrifice of praise to God, that is, the fruit of our lips, giving thanks to His name." When you praise God and thank Him for who He is and what He has done, you offer Him fruit.

Help to those in need is a third kind of fruit offered to God. Members of the Philippian church gave Paul a gift, and he told them he was glad for their sakes that they had: "Not that I seek the gift, but

I seek for the fruit that abounds to your account" (Phil. 4:17). He appreciated it not for the sake of the gift, but for the fruit in their lives.

In Romans 15:28, Paul writes, "Therefore, when I have performed this and have sealed to them this fruit, I shall go by way of you to Spain." Again he refers to a gift as "fruit." In both cases, believers' gifts revealed their love, so Paul counted those gifts as fruit. A gift to someone in need is fruit, if it is offered from a loving heart in the divine energy of the indwelling Christ.

Purity in conduct is another kind of spiritual fruit. Paul wanted Christians to be holy in their behavior. He encouraged the Colossians, "that you may walk worthy of the LORD, fully pleasing Him, being fruitful in every good work and increasing in the knowledge of God" (Col. 1:10).

Scripture says *converts* are another type of fruit. For example, Paul called the first converts in Achaia the "the firstfruits of Achaia" (1 Cor. 16:15; cf. Dan. 12:3; John 4:36; Rom. 6:22; 1 Cor. 3:5–9).

Like other spiritual fruit, success in winning converts is not accomplished by anxiously keeping busy in ministry, in this case engaging in lots of "evangelistic activities"—it comes by abiding in the Vine. The way to be effective in leading people to Christ is not solely by being aggressive; rather it is by abiding in Christ. Concentrate on your relationship to Jesus Christ, and He will give you opportunities to share your faith. There is no need to become anxious because you have not yet won a certain number of people to Christ. As you become closer to Him and more like Him, you will discover that sharing your faith is a natural outgrowth of abiding. You may not always see fruit immediately, but fruit will be borne, nevertheless.

When Jesus was traveling to Samaria, He met a woman getting water. She told the people in her town about Jesus. As the people from the town came out to meet Him, He said to the disciples,

"Do you not say, 'There are still four months and then comes the harvest'"? Behold, I say to you, lift up your eyes and look at the fields, for they are already white for harvest! And he who reaps receives wages, and gathers fruit for eternal life, that both he who sows and he who reaps may rejoice together. For in this the saying is true: 'One sows and another reaps.' I sent you to reap that for which you have not labored; others have labored, and you have entered into their labors." (John 4:35–38)

The disciples were reaping the results of other people's labor. Those people did not see all the results of their labor, but their efforts still bore fruit.

Modern missions pioneer William Carey spent thirty-five years in India before he saw one convert. Some people think he had a fruitless ministry. But almost every convert in India to this day is fruit on his branch, because he translated the whole New Testament into many different Indian dialects. Carey was not the one to reap what he had sown, but his life bore much fruit.

One of the most fulfilling experiences in life is to bear fruit for God. If it isn't happening in your life, the reason is simple—you are not abiding in the Vine.

ANSWERED PRAYER

God gives an incredible promise to those who abide: "'If you abide in Me, and My words abide in you, you will ask what you desire, and it shall be done for you'" (John 15:7).

There are two conditions to that promise. First, we must abide. The Greek word for "abide" is in the aorist tense, which indicates something that happened at one point in time and has permanent results. Again, "abide" refers to salvation and indicates that the promise is only for real believers.

Of course, in His sovereign wisdom, God sometimes answers the prayers of an unbeliever; but He does not obligate Himself to do so.

The promise of answered prayer is reserved only for those who abide in the True Vine.

Still, many who are true branches do not always get answers to their prayers. It may be because they are not meeting Jesus' second condition, which is, "If . . . My words abide in you."

"My words" doesn't mean only the individual words of Christ. Some people misuse red-letter Bibles because they regard the words of Jesus as more inspired or more important than the other words of Scripture. But the words of Paul, Peter, John, and Jude are just as important. The Lord Jesus Christ has spoken through the entirety of Scripture; *all* of it is His message to us. Therefore, when He says, "If . . . My words abide in you," He means we must have such high regard for all of Scripture that we let it abide in us, that we hide it in our hearts, and that we commit ourselves to knowing and obeying it.

To meet the first condition, a person must be a Christian. To meet the second condition, he must study all of Scripture to govern his life by what Christ has revealed.

As we saw in chapter 5 of our study, the same principle is found earlier in Jesus' discourse, "If you ask anything in My name, I will do it" (John 14:14). Christians who are abiding in Christ and controlled by His Word are not going to ask anything against God's will. Because they want what God wants, they are guaranteed answers to their prayers.

Our prayers will be answered if we follow Paul's example in 2 Corinthians 10:5, "[We are] casting down arguments and every high thing that exalts itself against the knowledge of God, bringing every thought into captivity to the obedience of Christ." We must rid our minds of everything that violates God's truth and will. When we think according to the will of God, we will pray according to the will of God and our prayers will be answered.

There is so little power in the prayers of the church today because we are not fully abiding in Christ and seeking His mind. Instead of bringing our minds into obedience to Christ and asking according to

His will, we ask selfishly; therefore our prayers go unanswered (James 4:3). If we cultivated an intimate love relationship with Christ, we would desire what He desires; and we would ask and receive.

The psalmist says, "Delight yourself also in the LORD, and He shall give you the desires of your heart" (Ps. 37:4). That means that when you delight completely in the Lord, He implants the right desires in your heart. His desires become yours. What a blessing it is to know that God can answer every prayer we bring to Him!

ABUNDANT LIFE

Abiding in Christ is the source of the abundant life Jesus speaks of in John 10:10, "I have come that they may have life, and that they may have it more abundantly." Those who abide fulfill the magnificent purpose of life, which is to give God all the glory He deserves. Jesus assured the disciples, "'By this My Father is glorified, that you bear much fruit'" (John 15:8). When a Christian abides, God can work through him to produce much fruit. Since God produces it, He is the one glorified.

Paul recognized the source of fruit in his life. He told the Roman Christians, "For I will not dare to speak of any of those things which Christ has not accomplished through me" (Rom. 15:18). He did not tell people how good he was at preaching or evangelism. He recognized that everything worthwhile in his life came from God. He declared to the church in Galatia, "I have been crucified with Christ; it is no longer I who live, but Christ lives in me" (Gal. 2:20). He knew God did it all.

Peter had the same idea in mind when he wrote, "having your conduct honorable among the Gentiles, that when they speak against you as evildoers, they may, by your good works which they observe, glorify God in the day of visitation" (1 Pet. 2:12).

So this is the believer's logical progression to enjoying the spiritually abundant life: the one who abides bears fruit; God is glorified in the fruit because He is the One who deserves credit for it; the purpose of life is fulfilled because God is glorified; and thus the one who abides and glorifies God experiences abundant life.

FULL JOY

One of the chief elements of the abundant life is fullness of joy, which is an outgrowth of abiding in the True Vine. Jesus says in John 15:11, "These things I have spoken to you, that My joy may remain in you, and that your joy may be full."

God wants us to be consumed with joy, but few Christians are. Churches have many people who are bitter, discontented, and complaining. Some people think the Christian life is monastic deprivation and drudgery—a bitter religious pill. But God has designed it for our joy. It is when we violate God's design that we lose our joy. If we abide fully, we will have full joy.

When David sinned, he no longer sensed the presence of God. He cried out, "Restore to me the joy of Your salvation" (Ps. 51:12). He had allowed sin to hinder his pure, abiding relationship with God. He did not lose his salvation, but he lost *the joy* of his salvation.

That joy returned when David confessed his sin to God and accepted the consequences of it. His guilt was removed; he returned to a pure, unhindered, abiding relationship with the Lord; and God made his joy full again.

As long as we abide wholeheartedly in the True Vine, our joy is unaffected by external circumstances, persecution, or the disappointments of life. We can experience the same constant joy Jesus had, because His joy flows through those who abide in Him.

SECURITY

Abiding in the True Vine brings the deepest kind of security. Romans 8:1 says, "There is therefore now no condemnation to those who are in Christ Jesus." Those who are in Him cannot be removed, they cannot be cut off, and they need not fear judgment. There is no suggestion here that those who now abide might later cease to do so. Their position is secure.

On the other hand, those who do not abide will be judged. Jesus warned, "'If anyone does not abide in Me, he is cast out as a branch and is withered; and they gather them and throw them into the fire, and they are burned'" (John 15:6). He is referring to the Judas-branches, the false disciples. Since they have no living connection to Jesus Christ, they are cast out.

The true believer, however, could never be thrown away. Jesus promises in John 6:37, "'All that the Father gives Me will come to Me, and the one who comes to Me I will by no means cast out.'" If a person is cast forth from the Vine, it is because his faith was not real in the first place.

The branches that are cast off are gathered and burned. They burn forever and ever. It is a tragic picture of God's final judgment.

Jesus' parable of the wheat and tares tells us that the angels of God gather those destined for judgment. "'The Son of Man will send out His angels, and they will gather out of His kingdom all things that offend, and those who practice lawlessness, and will cast them into the furnace of fire. There shall be wailing and gnashing of teeth'" (Matt. 13:41–42).

So there will be a day when God sends His angels to gather from around the world the Judas-branches who have no connection to Christ. He will cast them into eternal hell. It is tragic when a person appears to be a genuine branch but ends up in hell.

William Pope was a member of the Methodist Church in England for most of his life. He made a pretense of knowing Christ and served in many church capacities. His wife died a genuine believer.

Soon, however, he began to drift from Christ. He had companions who believed in the redemption of demons. He began going with them to the public house of prostitution. In time, he became a drunkard.

He admired the famous skeptic Thomas Paine and would assemble with Paine's friends on Sundays when they would confirm each other in their infidelity. They sometimes amused themselves by throwing the Bible on the floor and kicking it around.

Finally, Pope contracted tuberculosis. Someone visited him and told him of the great Redeemer. That person told Pope he could be saved from the punishment of his sins.

But Pope replied, "I have no contrition; I cannot repent. God will damn me! I know the day of grace is lost. God has said to such as me, 'I will laugh at your calamity, and mock when your fear cometh.' I have denied Him; my heart is hardened."

Then he cried, "Oh, the hell, the pain I feel! I have chosen my way. I have done the horrible damnable deed; I have crucified the Son of God afresh; I have counted the blood of the covenant an unholy thing! Oh that wicked and horrible thing of blaspheming the Holy Spirit, which I know that I have committed; I want nothing but hell! Come, oh devil, and take me!" (From John Myers, *Voices from the Edge of Eternity* [Old Tappan, N.J.: Spire Books, 1972], 147–49.)

William Pope had spent his whole life in the church, but his end was infinitely worse than his beginning. Every person must consider the two great alternatives: abide in the Vine and receive all of God's blessings in heaven, or refuse to believe and abide and thereby burn in hell forever.

It seems like an obvious choice, doesn't it? Yet millions of people reject God's offer of salvation, preferring the superficial relationship of the false branch. Perhaps you know people like that—or maybe you are like that yourself. If so, you and they need to embrace Jesus' loving invitation: "Abide in Me, and I in you" (John 15:4).

ELEVEN

HOW TO BE A FRIEND OF JESUS

ANCIENT ORIENTAL KINGS OFTEN RELIED ON A SELECT GROUP of advisers, special friends of the monarch, who functioned much like the cabinet of a modern American president. But those were far more than mere political consultants—they were his intimate friends. They protected and cared for him and were given immediate access to him—they could even enter his bedchamber. He valued their advice more than that of generals, statesmen, or rulers of other nations. No one was closer to the king.

The royal advisers' role was one that transcended the king-subject or master-disciple relationship. It was a position of intimate friendship, a bond of love and trust that superseded formality, protocol, or any external threat.

Jesus cultivated that kind of relationship with His disciples, and in His final words to them on the night before He died, He repeatedly affirmed that He valued the intimacy they shared. The time had come that He must leave them, but He wanted them to be sure of their status as His friends.

"This is My commandment, that you love one another as I have loved you. Greater love has no one than this, than to lay down one's life for his friends. You are My friends if you do whatever I command you. No longer do I call you servants, for a servant does not know what his master is doing; but I have called you friends, for all things that I heard from my Father I have made known to you. You did not choose Me, but I chose you and appointed you that you should go and bear fruit, and that your fruit should remain, that whatever you ask the Father in My name He may give you." (John 15:12–16)

The Greek word for "slave," or "servant," is *doulos*. In Jewish culture it did not have a negative connotation. The disciples would have been happy to be known as Jesus' slaves. To be a servant—especially a servant of God—was by no means a shameful thing.

But to be known as the friend of God was an honor. Abraham was the only one in the Old Testament upon whom God conferred the title. Everyone familiar with the Jewish Scriptures would have been aware of the uniqueness of Abraham's place as God's friend, so Jesus' words to the eleven remaining disciples must have utterly thrilled them. All of them had longed for intimacy with Him—they had even contended among themselves about which one would sit closest to Him in the kingdom. Now He reassured all of them that He too desired intimacy with them, and he listed a number of the characteristics essential to an intimate relationship with Him.

OBEDIENCE

The first characteristic is obedience, which sums up the essence of friendship with Christ. Actually, obedience is a condition for intimacy. In verse 10, Jesus says, "'If you keep My commandments, you will abide in My love.'" Then in verse 14 He adds, "'You are My friends if you do whatever I command you.'" That is not to say that friendship with Him is either earned or attained by any amount of human effort but rather that obedience is an identifying mark of the friends of Jesus.

In fact, those who obey God share intimacy with Jesus as members of the same family. Jesus had explained before that obedience is characteristic of all those in His spiritual family:

> Then His brothers and His mother came, and standing outside they sent to Him, calling Him. And a multitude was sitting around Him; and they said to Him, "Look, Your mother and Your brothers are outside seeking You."
>
> But He answered them, saying, "Who is My mother, or My brothers?" And He looked around in a circle at those who sat about Him, and said, "Here are My mother and My brothers! For whoever does the will of God is My brother and My sister and mother." (Mark 3:31–35)

Scripture also speaks of the relationship of believers with Jesus as that of sheep who follow their Shepherd. Jesus says in John 10:27, "'My sheep hear My voice, and I know them, and they follow Me.'" Again, intimacy depends on willing obedience. In every metaphor Jesus ever used to describe His relationship with His disciples, obedience was an essential condition. In John 8:31, He says, "'If you abide in My word, you are My disciples indeed.'" Intimacy with Jesus Christ is always built on a foundation of obedience, whether it is the intimacy of a sheep and a shepherd, a teacher and a disciple, family members, or simply friends.

First John 3:9–10 refers to that identifying mark of the family of God: "Whoever has been born of God does not sin, for His seed remains in him; and he cannot sin, because he has been born of God. In this the children of God and the children of the devil are manifest: Whoever does not practice righteousness is not of God, nor is he who does not love his brother."

A person does not become a child of God through obedience— that would make salvation depend on good works. Rather, obedience is proof that a person is intimately connected to Jesus Christ through faith. It does not qualify someone to be a child of God. It only demonstrates that he is one.

The same is true of being a friend of Jesus. John 15:14 says, "'You are My friends if you do whatever I command you.'" That does not mean that obeying makes you a friend of Jesus. But if you are one, it will be visible by your obedience.

LOVE FOR EACH OTHER

A second characteristic of friendship with Jesus is love for fellow believers: "'This is My commandment, that you love one another as I have loved you. Greater love has no one than this, than to lay down one's life for his friends'" (John 15:12–13). The friends of Jesus have a deep, sincere, and abiding love for other Christians.

Love is a great source of personal fulfillment, and the world is hungry for it. But friends of Jesus are the only ones who can truly experience the love the world is seeking. Unbelievers know nothing of the love believers can share, because it comes from a source they cannot know. Love is a fruit of the Spirit (Gal. 5:22). Romans 5:5 says, "The love of God has been poured out in our hearts by the Holy Spirit who was given to us." The Christian overflows with the love of God; he lives in it, and it lives in him.

You cannot be a true believer without having love for other believers: "He who says he is in the light, and hates his brother, is in darkness until now. He who loves his brother abides in the light, and there is no cause for stumbling in him. But he who hates his brother is in darkness and walks in darkness, and does not know where he is going, because the darkness has blinded his eyes" (1 John 2:9–11). John further explains: "Whoever believes that Jesus is the Christ is born of God; and everyone who loves Him who begot also loves him who is begotten of Him" (1 John 5:1).

That is not to say that if we ever fail to love another Christian to the fullest, it proves we are not true believers. A Christian may sometimes fail to love a brother or sister in Christ the way he should. But

John is not explaining exceptions to the rule—he is describing the general pattern believers follow.

It is natural for a true friend of Jesus to love other friends of Jesus. Paul writes, "But concerning brotherly love you have no need that I should write to you, for you yourselves are taught by God to love one another" (1 Thess. 4:9). To be unloving to another Christian, a Christian has to violate his new nature in Christ, resist the love that is natural to his new nature, and devise sin instead.

Jesus wants us to love just as He loves. He showed His deep desire when He said, "'This is My commandment, that you love one another *as I have loved you.* Greater love has no one than this, than to lay down one's life for his friends'" (John 15:12–13, emphasis added).

Of course our love cannot be on the same scale as His—He died for the sins of the world. But we can love the way He loves. We can be sacrificial and selfless. We can go beyond an external love and love with a love that is total and self-giving.

No fellow believer is a mere acquaintance. Whoever he or she is, we share a common spiritual heritage. We should see them as Christ sees them. Love should move us to give our wealth, to bear burdens, to feel what another feels, and to hurt where another hurts. We should be willing to comfort, to sacrifice, to instruct, and to support—just the way Christ would.

The quality of our love is our testimony for Christ. Because only Christians have God's love in their lives, the world should see the greatest love in Christians. Jesus says in John 13:35, "'By this all will know that you are My disciples, if you have love for one another.'"

The depth of sacrifice it is willing to make reveals the intensity of love. Giving up one's life has always been recognized as the supreme expression of love. Jesus was about to show He had that kind of love for His disciples. He told them, "'Greater love has no one than this, than to lay down one's life for his friends'" (John 15:13).

Too many who claim to know Christ are far from sacrificing their lives—they will not even give up a few minutes of time. Money is needed for ministries around the world, but the needs go unfulfilled because many Christians do not give sacrificially. Many who say they know the Lord will not even tell someone about Him, nor will they use their spiritual gifts to help another believer grow.

Christians fall far short of dying for others. Some have not even learned how to live for others. True love requires total sacrifice. When we love the way Christ did, the world will listen to our message. It is pointless to ask unbelievers to trust Christ when they cannot see His love operating in us.

Jesus sacrificed to the utmost, even for the unlovable. Paul says in Romans 5:7–8, "For scarcely for a righteous man will one die; yet perhaps for a good man someone would even dare to die. But God demonstrates His own love toward us, in that while we were still sinners, Christ died for us."

How do you know God loves you? Because He laid down His life. First John 3:16 says this: "By this we know love, because He laid down His life for us. And we also ought to lay down our lives for the brethren."

When my son Matt was very young, he would often say to me, "I love you, Dad." I would ask him, "How much do you love me?" He would answer, "I love you big much." I would ask, "How much is big much?" He would jump into my lap, put his arms around my neck, squeeze as tight as he could, and say, "That's big much."

If we could ask God, "How much do you love me?" I believe He would answer by pointing to a rocky hillside outside Jerusalem and saying, "Do you see the cross in the middle? My Son is on it. I love you that much."

Are you ready to lay down your life for another? Do you love sacrificially? Are you caring for the needs of others? Needs are all around you. Some people need to be taught; some need reproof; others need restoration. There are physical needs, and many people need prayer. We say we love people, but do we meet their needs?

Love is always practical. The Apostle John asks, "But whoever has this world's goods, and sees his brother in need, and shuts up his heart from him, how does the love of God abide in him?" (1 John 3:17). John then encourages the children of God to prove their love in an active way: "My little children, let us not love in word or in tongue, but in deed and truth" (v. 18). The true friend of Jesus meets the needs of others.

A KNOWLEDGE OF DIVINE TRUTH

In Jesus' day, slaves and their masters were rarely friends. They were not necessarily enemies—they simply did not cultivate the kind of relationship friends would have. A slave was told only what he should do, never why he should do it. He never knew his master's plans, goals, or feelings. He was merely a functionary who did what he was told, a living tool rarely included in the sharing of rewards.

It was different between Jesus and His disciples. He told them, "'No longer do I call you servants, for a servant does not know what his master is doing; but I have called you friends, for all things that I heard from my Father I have made known to you'" (John 15:15).

Surrender to Jesus Christ is never blind obedience. He shares with His friends everything He has received from the Father. They share His heart for His work because they know the whole plan from beginning to end. It is the truest kind of friendship. If we are His friends, we want what He wants, and we do His will because it is our heart's desire.

Jesus promised the disciples special insight. "'If you abide in My word, you are My disciples indeed. And you shall know the truth, and the truth shall make you free'" (John 8:31–32). Everything the Father told Him, He passed on to them. Consider His prayer to the Father: "'I have manifested Your name to the men whom You have given Me out of the world. They were Yours, You gave them to Me, and they have kept Your word. Now they have known that all things which You have given Me are from You. For I have given to them the words which You have given Me; and they have received them, and have known surely that I came forth from You; and they have believed that You sent Me'" (John 17:6–8).

Through His parables Jesus taught the disciples the mysteries of God's plan. Matthew writes, "And the disciples came and said to Him, 'Why do You speak to them in parables?' And He answered and said to them, 'Because it has been given to you to know the mysteries of the kingdom of heaven, but to them it has not been given'" (Matt. 13:10–11).

As a result, the disciples had special knowledge others sought but never found. Jesus told them, "'Blessed are the eyes which see the things you see; for I tell you that many prophets and kings have desired to see what you see, and have not seen it, and to hear what you hear, and have not heard it'" (Luke 10:23–24).

So spiritual knowledge passed from the Father through Jesus to the apostles. The apostles have passed it to us through the Scriptures. Paul writes in Romans 16:25–26 of "the mystery kept secret since the world began but now made manifest, and by the prophetic Scriptures made known to all nations, according to the commandment of the everlasting God, for obedience to the faith."

Spiritual understanding sets Christians apart. The things of God are spiritually discerned, and the unredeemed mind cannot understand them (1 Cor. 2:12–16). A philosopher or scientist who seeks spiritual truth apart from the Word of God and the Spirit of God knows little compared to the simplest Christian.

Jesus did not expect His disciples to follow Him without knowing where He was leading; they were not to be enslaved to a mechanical kind of obedience. They were to be His friends, and He revealed to them the truth He could not share with those not intimate with Him.

A DIVINE APPOINTMENT

Another characteristic of Jesus' friends is that they have been chosen by God and appointed to a position of service. Friendships are usually formed when two people choose to befriend each other. But a friendship with Jesus Christ is formed at His initiative. Jesus chose twelve men to be His disciples—they did not volunteer. Luke 6:13 records, "And when it was day, He called His disciples to Himself; and from them He chose twelve whom He also named apostles."

Jesus reminded the disciples, "'You did not choose Me, but I chose you and appointed you that you should go and bear fruit, and that your fruit should remain'" (John 15:16). He further told them, "'I chose you out of the world'" (v. 19). The Greek word for "chose" is *tithemi,* and in several places in the New Testament it is translated "appoint," or "ordain."

Paul uses the word in 1 Corinthians 12:28, where he says, "And God has appointed these in the church: first apostles, second prophets, third teachers." He uses it again in 2 Timothy 1:11, where he refers to the gospel as the message "to which I was appointed a preacher, an apostle, and a teacher."

In both places, Paul is referring to being chosen to specific service. In fact, throughout Scripture, wherever the doctrine of God's sovereign choice, or election, is discussed, the context always goes beyond salvation. That's because whenever God elects someone to salvation, He also ordains him or her to special service. Therefore, the friends of Jesus are not chosen just for salvation; they are chosen to do something: "I chose you and appointed you that you should go and bear fruit" (John 15:16). We have not been chosen to stand and watch the world go by.

I was once speaking at a conference of university students and met a young man who had dropped out of seminary. When I asked him what he was doing in the Lord's service, he said he was involved in a Bible study group he hoped would grow into a church. "We just have a little fellowship up here and praise God together," he said, with emphasis. I asked who taught them. He replied, "Nobody teaches us; we just share. No one ever teaches." I then asked, "What do you feel is your purpose?" "Well," he said, "we just praise the Lord a lot."

I asked if they were involved in evangelism. "No," he said, "we've been in existence two and a half years and we've never told anyone. We don't feel we are called to that. We are still an infant church, so we don't think we need to evangelize."

He had the idea they were called to sit with each other and sing. It is good to praise God and fellowship, but we are also called to go. The world will not come to us—we must go to it.

The Bible does not command those who are in the world to come to church. It commands those in the church to "'Go out into the highways and hedges, and compel them to come in'" (Luke 14:23). Jesus' last commission to His followers was, "'Go into all the world and preach the gospel to every creature'" (Mark 16:15).

He promised the disciples, "'You shall receive power when the Holy Spirit has come upon you; and you shall be witnesses to Me in Jerusalem, and in all Judea and Samaria, and to the end of the earth'" (Acts 1:8).

Jesus chose a group of men out of the world of darkness. He saved them, loved them, and trained them. He called them His friends. Then He sent them back into the world to tell it about Jesus Christ.

We have the high calling to glorify the name of Christ in the world. We are called and ordained to let God work His perfect will through us. Thus, life has purpose for the Christian. When we communicate the gospel and a person responds by receiving Christ, we have witnessed a Spirit-energized transformation that will last for eternity. It is so different from the unbeliever, whose life dwindles away without meaning, day after day with no eternal results. The Christian's life makes ripples throughout eternity because his fruit remains. Revelation 14:13 says of the dead in Christ, "'They may rest from their labors, and their works follow with them.'"

John 15:16 concludes with a promise from Jesus, "'Whatever you ask the Father in My name He may give you.'" As we have seen before, that is not a blanket promise to fulfill any request that we utter, just as long as we attach the magic words "in Jesus' name." It means we must ask the Father for the things Jesus would want. We cannot use prayer as a way to satisfy our lusts. We must be unselfish if we are to ask in His name. Praying in His name means asking according to God's will. If we do that, the answer is guaranteed.

We who have trusted in His name are all friends of Jesus Christ. We are not like subjects who crowd the streets, hoping to catch a glimpse of the king as he passes by. We have the right to enter His presence any time. We are the people closest to our King. It is thrilling to know we are the personal friends of the Creator and King of the universe.

People are either friends of Jesus Christ or friends of the world. Friendship with the world is hostility toward God. Friendship with Jesus Christ is intimacy with God. It is fellowship with the Trinity. It is unspeakable joy and full of glory. Such blessings, if they are not already yours, can belong to you today. But you must repent of your sins, renounce the world, and respond to Christ's call to be your Lord and Savior—and your Friend.

TWELVE

HATED WITHOUT A CAUSE

ABOUT TWENTY YEARS AGO, BOB MARRIOT, A YOUNG MAN from the college department at my church in southern California, was attacked and beaten while he was giving out tracts in a park. It was a brutal beating, but Bob recovered, and it was no time until he was back on the streets, telling people about Christ. He had not lost any of his zeal for the Lord.

A few weeks later Bob was witnessing for Christ at Seventh and Broadway in downtown Los Angeles, at 4:40 in the afternoon, when he was attacked and beaten again. This time, the back of his skull was fractured in four places. At the hospital, doctors drilled three holes in his skull to relieve the pressure, but they were unsuccessful, and three days later Bob died. He was committed to proclaiming Jesus Christ to a Christ-hating world, and he paid for it with his life.

That incident helped to change my perspective on the cost of serving Christ in a hostile world. It is too easy to have a casual attitude toward persecution when we read about how it affects believers in other parts of the world. But when it strikes close to home, it is a much more sobering experience.

When Luke recorded Jesus' command in Acts 1:8 that we are to be His "witnesses," he used the Greek word *martus,* from which we get the word *martyr*. Although it originally meant "witness," so many in the early church who witnessed for Christ were killed that the word came to refer primarily to a person who died for his testimony for Christ.

Jesus wanted the disciples to know they would meet hostility when they witnessed for Him. But on the night before He died, His purpose was primarily to comfort and reassure them. The bulk of His discourse that night consisted of words of comfort and encouragement. He saved until last what He had to say about the persecution they would face after He left.

Jesus told the disciples of His love (John 13). He gave them tremendous promises (chap. 14). He promised He was going to prepare a place for them and that He would return to take them there (vv. 2–3); told them that they would do greater works than He had done (v. 12); said they could ask anything in His name and He would do it (v. 13); promised that the Holy Spirit would live in them and be their Comforter (v. 16, KJV); reassured them they would be intensely loved by Him and by the Father (v. 23); said the disciples would possess divine life and knowledge (v. 26); and promised to give His peace (v. 27).

Next Jesus told the disciples they would bear fruit for God (John 15:5). He promised that they would abide and be closely connected to Him (v. 10); that they would have His joy (v. 11); and that His life would flow through them. Finally, He called them His friends (v. 14).

Then Christ had to warn His closest friends. Those men needed to know that, in spite of the wonderful divine promises that would be fulfilled in their lives, life would not be completely blissful. Ministry would not be easy in a rebellious, Christ-hating world. The world was going to treat them the same way it treated Him, and they were going to be despised and persecuted—even killed.

"These things I command you, that you love one another.

"If the world hates you, you know that it hated Me before it hated you. If you were of the world, the world would love its own. Yet because you are not of the world, but I chose you out of the world, therefore the world hates you. Remember the word that I said to you, 'A servant is not greater than his master.' If they persecuted Me, they will also persecute you. If they kept My word, they will keep yours also. But all these things they will do to you for My name's sake, because they do not know Him who sent Me. If I had not come and spoken to them, they would have no sin, but now they have no excuse for their sin. He who hates Me hates My Father also. If I had not done among them the works which no one else did, they would have no sin; but now they have seen and also hated both Me and My Father. But this happened that the word might be fulfilled which is written in their law, 'They hated Me without a cause.'" (John 15:17–25)

Verse 17 is Jesus' transition from describing His love for the disciples to describing the world's hatred: "'These things I command you, that you love one another.'" The Greek indicates a continuous action: "Keep on loving each other." He is saying, "Devote yourselves to one another and sacrifice for one another—love each other the way I loved you."

One reason their love for each other was so important was that the world would know nothing but hatred for them. Love for each other was the only love they would ever know. In a hostile world, they desperately needed love from each other.

History shows that the apostles were hated, just as Jesus predicted. James was martyred. The Roman emperor Nero beheaded Paul. Andrew persisted in preaching and was tied to a cross and crucified. Peter, too, was crucified, although traditionally it is held that he was crucified upside down because he did not consider himself worthy of the same death as His Savior. All of them were martyred, except perhaps Matthew and John, who was exiled to the Isle of Patmos. The rest of Christ's followers suffered persecution from the Roman government, which regarded them as disloyal citizens and a threat to the unity of the empire.

Rome was concerned about unity because the empire stretched from the Euphrates River to England and from Germany to North Africa. It included the widest variety of peoples and cultures imaginable. Such a multicultural empire could easily become divided. Roman officials viewed worship of the emperor as a way to bond the different peoples of the vast empire.

All Roman citizens were required to worship Caesar. Once a year, they had to demonstrate their allegiance by burning a pinch of incense to the supposed deity of Caesar. Then they were required to shout, "Caesar is Lord." As long as they worshiped the emperor, citizens could worship any other god they wished.

But Christians would call no man Lord, so the government considered them irresponsible and disloyal and persecuted them from time to time. Mobs added to the persecution by the government. People in various parts of the empire hated the Christians because they did not fit into society.

Christians were accused of cannibalism because they talked about eating the flesh and drinking the blood of Christ at their communion services. Some accused the Christians of immorality, thinking the Christian "love feast" was an orgy. Because Christians expected the second coming of their King, some thought they were planning a rebellion. They were suspected of arson because they said God was going to bring fire on judgment day. (They were blamed for the burning of Rome in the first century.)

Though the specific misunderstandings may differ, the same hostility toward Christians is true of today's world. The world does not accept Christians, because it rejects their Lord. And the world's hostility is not something we can evade without compromising. Jesus gives three main reasons sufferings and persecutions are unavoidable for Christians.

CHRIST'S FOLLOWERS ARE NOT OF THE WORLD

First of all, Jesus' disciples are rejected by the world because they are no longer a part of the world's system. Jesus told the apostles, "'If you were of the world, the world would love its own. Yet because you are not of the world, but I chose you out of the world, therefore the world hates you'" (John 15:19). They had been called out; because they were different, they no longer could fit into the world's system. "World" is the English translation of *kosmos,* a common word in Greek. It appears often in John's writings and changes its meaning with the context. Here it means the evil, sinful system begun by Satan and acted out by men. The *kosmos* (usually simply transliterated *cosmos* in English) is the result and expression of human depravity. It is set against Christ, His people, and His kingdom, and Satan and his evil minions control it.

This evil world system is incapable of genuine love. When Jesus said the world loves its own, He was not saying that worldly beings love each other. "Its own" is not a masculine plural, which would indicate a love directed toward other people. The word in the Greek text is neuter plural, meaning that the people caught up in the world love their own things. A worldly individual loves himself and his own things. He loves others only if it is to his advantage. The world's love is always selfish, superficial, and interested only in its own advantage.

The cosmos is against those who love and follow Jesus, those who declare their faith in Him and show it by their words and deeds. It does not persecute those who are part of its system. Jesus said to His earthly brothers, who did not follow Him during His ministry, "'The world cannot hate you, but it hates Me because I testify of it that its works are evil'" (John 7:7).

People living in the world who do not know Jesus Christ are part of a system that is anti-God, anti-Christ, and satanic. That system militates against God and His principles and is opposed to all that is good, godly, and Christlike. Yet I am always amazed at how easily some Christians believe the world is tolerant of God and Jesus.

It is true that the world is religious, but religion is not the same as righteousness. False religions have a superficial tolerance of the things of God. Still, they are tools of Satan in his war against the truth. They disguise themselves with godliness, but they reveal their true nature by suppressing the truth. Throughout history, false religion has been the most aggressive opponent of the true church.

Persecution is inevitable for righteous people living in the world. Paul warned Timothy, "Yes, and all who desire to live godly in Christ Jesus will suffer persecution" (2 Tim. 3:12). It is an inescapable fact of godly living. But because many people who attend church are not personally antagonized, they feel the world does not oppose true Christians. It may be, however, that they get no opposition from the world because it is not obvious they are Christians.

Or perhaps they are not genuine Christians at all. The true believer stands apart from the world because he has been made holy through identification with Jesus Christ. He lives righteously and does not belong to the system. Because a genuine Christian represents God and Christ, Satan uses the world's system to attack him. That is why Jesus prayed for the Father's protection of His followers: "I do not pray that You should take them out of the world, but that You should keep them from the evil one" (John 17:15).

Our lives are to be a rebuke to the sinful world. Ephesians 5:11 says, "And have no fellowship with the unfruitful works of darkness, but rather expose *them.*" One of the reasons we do not feel as much hatred from the world as we should is that our lives are not a rebuke. To live in a hostile and perverted world, we must be blameless. Paul, writing to the Philippian Christians, cautioned them to avoid sin, "that you may become blameless and harmless, children of God without fault in the midst of a crooked and perverse generation, among whom you shine as lights in the world" (Phil. 2:15).

Romans 1:32 describes people in the world's immoral system by saying that they not only do evil themselves but "give hearty approval" (NASB) to others who do it. Some people love those who are more wicked than they because it makes them feel more righteous. When the Christian's life rebukes their sinfulness, they become hostile.

But Jesus has called us to that kind of confrontation. We cannot sit in our churches and expect unbelievers to sense that they are indicted. The early church did not put up a sign saying, "Revival: All Unsaved Come in on Weekdays and Feel Condemned." It should not be necessary for people to come into our church to see that we are Christians. Our lives should show it. Jesus says in Matthew 5:14 that we should be like a city that can be seen for miles because it is set on a hill. In the next verse He says that believers are like a lamp that should not be put under a basket but rather should be set on a lampstand so that it can light the entire house. Our righteousness must be visible to the world, not hidden in a church building.

We stand out from the world because Jesus has chosen us. In John 15:19 He says, "'I chose you out of the world.'" The word "chose" is in the Greek middle voice, which gives it a reflexive meaning. Jesus is literally saying, "'I chose you for Myself.'" He has chosen us to be different. We are called to be a living rebuke to the rest of the world.

Satan does not like to lose anyone, and thus he moves to attack the child of God. Peter warns Christians, "Your adversary, the devil, prowls about like a roaring lion, seeking someone to devour" (1 Pet. 5:8, NASB). Satan pursues Christians and sets the whole world in motion against them. He hates the righteous as much as he hates God, for both God and the righteous stand for the same thing.

I once participated in an intensive evangelization of a local university campus. We shared the gospel with several thousand students. The next day the college newspaper said that unless the organization sponsoring the evangelistic effort complied with university policy and discontinued its evangelistic work, "direct action [would] be taken against [it]." The dean had received complaints from students who were "accosted" and asked to enter into discussions. The dean cited campus policy that forbade using "university facilities . . . for religious conversion." In other words, it was wrong for students to get saved on that campus—it was against the rules. And no amount of discussion with campus officials could get them to see the inequity of their rules.

That is an example of the way the world system resists people who want to tell the truth about sin. Anyone was free to go on that same campus and convert people to Communism. And no one objected if students organized for any other cause, no matter how bizarre. But when you told people about Jesus Christ, you broke the rules. The world does not want to be confronted with the truth.

THE WORLD HATED OUR LORD

A second reason persecution is inevitable for Christians is that the world desperately hates the Lord Jesus. Jesus told the eleven, " 'Remember the word that I said to you, 'A servant is not greater than his master.' If they persecuted Me, they will also persecute you. If they kept My word, they will keep yours also' " (John 15:20). Because the world hates Him, it hates those of us who name Him as Lord.

Not everyone rejects Christ, and not everyone will reject us. A few will listen and believe. Yet much of the world's apparent acceptance of Jesus is nothing more than a facade. Most of the movies, songs, and books about Jesus written from a secular viewpoint only confuse and deceive people into thinking they understand the truth about Jesus. But no one can really know Him unless he or she knows something about sin and repentance.

There was a time in history when Christianity became a fad. It had survived some two centuries of intense persecution, and then the Roman government suddenly accepted it. Christianity became the official religion of the Roman Empire, and everyone wanted to be "a Christian." True Christianity was endangered at least as much by the shallow popularity that resulted from those developments as it had been by persecution. Because everyone was calling himself a Christian, no one understood how a believer's life was distinctive or what Christianity really stood for. Christianity had become a monstrosity, an institutionalized blasphemy, and it became unclear just what constituted genuine faith. Satan welcomes that kind of confusion as much as he relishes persecuting the church.

There is a unique joy in being so identified with Jesus Christ that you suffer the rebuke, ridicule, and hatred directed at Him. Most Christians do not know that joy. In Philippians 3:10, Paul calls it "the fellowship of His sufferings." First Peter 2:21 says, "For to this you were called, because Christ also suffered for us, leaving us an example, that you should follow His steps." But when we share His sufferings, we also share His joy over those who come to saving faith. And that makes all the sacrifices worthwhile.

THE WORLD DOES NOT KNOW GOD

Jesus told the disciples another reason persecution must come: "'But all these things they will do to you for My name's sake, because they do not know Him who sent Me'" (John 15:21). The Jews of Jesus' day prided themselves on what they thought was an in-depth knowledge of God. When Jesus said that they did not know God, the religious leaders were infuriated. But in rejecting Christ they themselves proved He was right. They claimed to know God, yet they hated Christ, who was God in human flesh. Their love for God was a pretense.

What many people fail to realize is that religion itself is perhaps the greatest hindrance to the knowledge of the true God. The world's approach to religion is to postulate a god and worship him, even though that god does not exist outside man's imagination. Jesus exposed the false religion propounded by the Jewish leaders when He said, "'You are of your father the devil, and the desires of your father you want to do'" (John 8:44).

The problem is not that men have no access to the truth about God. Romans 1:19 says, "Because what may be known of God is manifest in them, for God has shown it to them." Through both innate knowledge and nature, God gives everyone basic knowledge that He exists. People willfully reject the truth, not because of ignorance but because they love the darkness rather than the light. Exposing men to the truth is like shining a light on an insect—the bug just wants to crawl back into the darkness.

God gave the Jews of Jesus' day the Old Testament and the Messiah. They heard what Christ said and saw what He did. But they killed Him. They rejected everything God could reveal to them. It was the one sin for which there could be no remedy. After seeing Him cast out a demon, a group of Pharisees said, "This fellow does not cast out demons except by Beelzebub, the ruler of the demons" (Matt. 12:24). Their rejection of Him was complete and irreversible. They were rejecting the fullest possible revelation.

Jesus then warned the Jewish leaders, "'Every sin and blasphemy will be forgiven men, but the blasphemy against the Spirit will not be forgiven men'" (v. 31). He had done everything through the Holy Spirit. In rejecting Him and attributing His works to Satan's power, they were blaspheming the Spirit. They could not be forgiven because they had rejected full revelation. There was nothing more they could see or hear that would change their rejection.

Jesus quotes Psalms 35:19 and 69:4 in John 15:25 "'They hated Me without a cause.'" There was no reason for the Jews to reject Christ. Their rejection of Him was a fulfillment of David's words. That does not mean God desired that they would hate Jesus; but He planned that their hatred of Him would be completely without cause. Jesus had healed all manner of diseases; He had fed multitudes; He had been completely sinless. There was no reason for anyone to hate Him.

The world hated Jesus because He exposed its sin. When His divine holiness shone on those of the world, it revealed their love of darkness. Instead of turning to Him in faith and love, they turned against Him in hatred.

The world is no different today—it still hates Jesus. And it still hates those who truly serve Him. If you are going to follow Him, you will have to suffer the hatred of the world. If you are unwilling, you cannot be His disciple. The price may seem high, but the rewards are higher.

Suffering for Christ's sake is the calling of every believer (2 Tim. 3:12). He does not call any of us to a life without suffering or persecution. Suffering is a part of the cost everyone must count if he wants to be a disciple.

Still, to be persecuted for Him is a unique privilege. It is a special joy to be identified with Christ in His suffering (Phil. 3:10). And when we truly suffer for righteousness' sake—when we are willing to be hated without a cause—that will be when we begin to understand persecution not as a thing to be resisted or avoided but as a wonderful aspect of our fellowship with Christ.

All in all, Jesus has left us quite a blueprint for how to survive and prosper in a world of unbelievers. He gave us the supreme example of humble love when He washed the disciples feet. And He left us a complete array of promises and challenges that only He could pledge: the hope of heaven; the promises of the Holy Spirit, spiritual power, supply, truth, peace, fruitfulness, joy; and even the guarantee that we will have persecution.

All of those things are ours, because the Lord Jesus Christ is ours. Consider again His gracious words: "'I will not leave you orphans; I will come to you. A little while longer and the world will see Me no more, but you will see Me. Because I live, you will live also. At that day you will know that I am in My Father, and you in Me, and I in you'" (John 14:18–20). Jesus was going away in physical form, but He was going to be with the disciples in spiritual form. Even today, He dwells in every single believer with His own marvelous presence.

STUDY GUIDE

CHAPTER 1
THE HUMILITY OF LOVE

Summarizing the Chapter

In contrast to the contemporary emphasis on pride and self-esteem, Jesus' washing of the disciples' feet provides us with the supreme example of loving humility and service to others.

Getting Started (Choose One)

1. Is the problem of an overemphasis on pride and self-esteem as bad within the church as it is in secular society? If not, do you think it ever will be? If it is as bad, why? What influences make the problem what it is?
2. What daily, mundane challenge in our culture do you find most difficult or tiring? How is it a parallel to the ancient need for foot washing and the way the disciples failed to respond to that task? Elaborate on your answer.

Answering the Questions

1. What major transition does John 13 mark in Jesus' earthly ministry?
2. Why would the feet of Jesus and the disciples have been so dirty when they reached the upper room?
3. What was perhaps the lowliest duty slaves in Bible times had to perform?
4. What prevented the disciples from taking care of the foot-washing task in the upper room (see Luke 22:24–26)?
5. What does the Greek expression *eis telos* mean? How does it characterize Jesus' love for others? Give some examples.
6. What statement is a good, concise summary of the theme of 1 Corinthians 13?
7. What, other than his betrayal of Jesus, was so tragic about Judas Iscariot's experience as a "disciple"? How does it help us to better understand the magnitude of Jesus' love?
8. What character traits are most prominent in canceling out one's capacity for love and humility?
9. What is necessary for love to be genuine?
10. When Jesus taught Peter, what pattern of instruction found elsewhere in the Gospel of John did He follow?
11. What must happen to anyone who wants a saving relationship with Jesus?
12. What verse toward the end of the New Testament restates the essence of spiritual foot washing?
13. What do some denominations believe John 13:12–17 is teaching? Is that actually the intent of the passage? What is the real lesson Jesus wants us to follow?

Focusing on Prayer

*   Prayerfully allow the Holy Spirit to examine your heart and point out areas of pride and self-centeredness that remain in

your life. Ask God to help you replace them with traits of love and humility.

- Pray for the opportunity to perform an act of loving and humble service for another believer or group of believers.

Applying the Truth

Memorize 1 John 1:9 or 3:18.

CHAPTER 2
UNMASKING THE BETRAYER

Summarizing the Chapter

The story of Judas Iscariot is the ultimate tragedy, involving perhaps the most despised figure in human history. It culminates in John 13:18–30 by displaying the absolute contrast of good (Jesus) and evil (Judas) and teaching us what it means to forfeit the greatest of spiritual opportunities by stubbornly clinging to sinful desires and evil priorities.

Getting Started (Choose One)

1. If you can, think of an example from your own experience or the news events of your lifetime of a particularly tragic story. Describe it briefly and tell why you think it's noteworthy or comparable to Judas' story.
2. Jesus was extremely patient and longsuffering with Judas over the three years they were together. How many "second chances" are too many? Concerning what issues would you refuse to grant someone another opportunity? Why? What might make you change your mind?

Answering the Questions

1. What bizarre apocryphal story vividly illustrates the extreme contempt many in the early centuries of the church had for Judas?

2. By the end of his life, what sins particularly characterized Judas?

3. For how much did Judas agree with the Jewish leaders to betray Jesus? What did that amount equal in those days?

4. Following the foot washing, why did Jesus tell the disciples about His impending betrayal?

5. For what reasons did the Father and the Son choose Judas to betray Jesus?

6. What did the Old Testament prophesy about Judas' actions in betraying Christ? Cite at least two references.

7. What in the form of a warning is a primary lesson we can learn from the example of Judas Iscariot?

8. What wrong conclusions might the eleven disciples have drawn after hearing about Jesus' upcoming betrayal? But what should they have understood from John 13:20?

9. What does the presence of hypocrites in the church fail to diminish or hinder among real believers? What bearing does the parable of the wheat and tares have on this situation (Matt. 13:24–30)?

10. List some reasons that Judas' betrayal would have caused anguish within Jesus' heart.

11. Describe the seating arrangement Jesus and the disciples used in the upper room. How did that affect the interaction between certain disciples concerning Judas' situation?

12. What kind of dip was used along with the unleavened bread at the Passover meal? What did it signify when the host gave a dipped morsel of bread to someone else at the meal?

13. Why did salvation for Judas finally become impossible (see Heb. 6:4–6)?

14. How did the other disciples misunderstand what was happening when Jesus sent Judas away? What was the true significance of His statement, "What you do, do quickly" (John 13:27)?

Focusing on Prayer

• Pray for the people in your church that they would have pure hearts and be free from hypocrisy.

• Thank God for your relationship to Christ and pray that His Spirit would strengthen it and increase your love for the Savior more each day.

Applying the Truth

Spend some extended time reading and studying the story of Absalom in 2 Samuel 13:23–19:8. In what ways were Absalom and Ahithophel similar to Judas? Different from him? What additional lessons about hypocrisy, treachery, and pride can you draw from that account? What sin do you need to be most on guard against as you serve the Lord?

CHAPTER 3
THE MARKS OF THE COMMITTED CHRISTIAN

Summarizing the Chapter

In John 13:31–38, Jesus sets forth the three vital, distinguishing characteristics that should identify every genuine believer: an unending preoccupation with God's glory, an unfailing love for other believers, and an unswerving loyalty to Christ.

Getting Started (Choose One)

1. What is your opinion of the various external symbols (bumper stickers, tee shirts with slogans or verses, etc.) people use to identify themselves as followers of Christ? Do you use any of them? Why or why not?
2. Many well-known products (foods, beverages, cars, clothing) have characteristics that everyone recognizes. Which products like this come to mind for you? How have their identifying marks influenced your brand loyalty? Are there some brands you will never switch from?

Answering the Questions

1. What is the core reason for which a Christian should live?
2. What aspects of Christ's death on the cross make it the greatest, most glorious work in the history of the universe?
3. What is one of the best ways believers can glorify God?
4. What is another, better-known term for the components of God's glory?
5. Which attribute of God stands out at the Cross above all others?
6. When will the greatest glory of Christ occur? What is necessary for that to be accomplished?
7. What missionary to India was preeminently concerned with the glory of Christ?
8. What system does love eliminate the need for (see Rom. 13:8–10)?
9. Why do various sects and false doctrines have such influence today? What is especially lacking among Christians that otherwise could prevent such confusion?
10. What are two key ways believers can demonstrate visible love?
11. How will a genuine, practiced loyalty manifest itself in the lives of Christ's disciples?

12. In what four ways did Peter temporarily fail the test of loyalty to Jesus?

Focusing on Prayer

- Reflect on the areas in which you are strong and weak in identifying as a Christian. Pray that God would help you to be strong in every area of discipleship.
- Thank the Lord that Christ was glorified after His ascension, and that you too can anticipate future glory.

Applying the Truth

If necessary, seek out a person in your church who needs your forgiveness or who needs to forgive you. Prior to doing this, prayerfully plan what you will say and use Scripture from this chapter to assist you in making things right. Thank the Lord for what the results will be. Meditate on Philippians 2:3–4 as a basis for your words and actions.

CHAPTER 4
THE SOLUTION TO A TROUBLED HEART

Summarizing the Chapter

John 14:1–6 is the basis for Christ's true comfort, by means of simple, trusting faith in our Lord's faithful presence, His trustworthy promises of heaven, and the truth of His divine person, which provides the only path to salvation.

Getting Started (Choose One)

1. Our commercialized world advertises many offers of comfort. Which one or ones do you think lure the most people into a false sense of security? What are the most alluring ones for you? Why?

2. Based on pictures you've seen, or actual visits you've made, which city in the world do you consider the most beautiful? What features should a city have to be attractive? Explain.

Answering the Questions

1. Who viewed John 14:1–6 as the most valuable and comforting sermon Jesus ever preached on earth?

2. Why were the disciples so upset and focused on themselves as they listened to Jesus in the upper room?

3. What had reinforced the disciples' one-sided view of Messiah's role and raised their hopes unduly?

4. What basic Old Testament tenet about God, which the disciples would have been familiar with, was Jesus placing Himself on a par with and reminding them of in John 14:1?

5. How is Jesus' invisible presence more advantageous to us than is His visible presence?

6. List three of the four common New Testament synonyms for heaven. What is the special connotation of each?

7. Why is "dwelling places" a more accurate translation than "mansions" in John 14:2?

8. When translated to miles (from Rev. 21:16), how big is heaven in square miles and cubic miles?

9. What kind of materials make up the construction of heaven (see Rev. 21:18–22)?

10. Why should the Christian not be afraid of death?

Focusing on Prayer

- Praise and thank God that Jesus is the perfect comforter and always present when you need Him.
- Ask the Lord to make you more conscious of and excited about the prospect of heaven. And pray for opportunities to share this renewed excitement with others.

Applying the Truth

Memorize Deuteronomy 31:6 or 1 Peter 1:8.

CHAPTER 5
JESUS IS GOD

Summarizing the Chapter

In John 14:7–14, Jesus continues His ministry of comfort to the disciples by reaffirming His deity; promising that after He goes to the Father they will witness a newer, larger scope of His power; and guaranteeing to meet all their needs, consistent with His character and will.

Getting Started (Choose One)

1. Every year, the prominent secular news magazines have one or two cover stories devoted to some "new finding" that is skeptical about who Jesus was, what Paul really taught, the reliability of the Bible, etc. Do you ever read these articles? Is there any value in them at all? Why or why not?
2. Have you ever felt at a loss or sad when a long-time favorite boss, teacher, or pastor retired or moved away? Did others involved share those feelings? How did you cope with the change?

Answering the Questions

1. What is the single most important issue any fair-minded person must resolve concerning the person of Jesus?

2. What was the basic error of Sabellius' teaching about who Jesus was?

3. According to Jesus, what would have prevented the disciples' confusion and uncertainty about God the Father?

4. What impending events would help the disciples to better understand the relationship of Jesus to the Father?

5. What did Philip's question in John 14:8 reveal about him?

6. Why is it wrong and even dangerous to make supernatural manifestations the basis for Christianity's authenticity?

7. What elements constituted the factual basis for the disciples' faith? What were they doing with that information when they questioned Jesus the night before His death?

8. In what sense were the disciples' works eventually greater than Jesus' works? What helped make that true?

9. What is not meant by the concept of praying in Jesus' name? What does it actually involve, and how should that influence our praying?

Focusing on Prayer

- You might know someone whose faith is wavering. Pray that they would turn back to Scripture and realize afresh the wonderful revealed truths that are the bases of Christianity.

- Give thanks that you have access by faith to the spiritual power Christ made possible by sending us the indwelling Holy Spirit.

Applying the Truth

For more insight on the deity of Christ, read and study John 1:1–18 or Colossians 1:9–20. What parallels or additional material do you see in that passage compared to John 14:7–14?

CHAPTER 6
THE HOLY SPIRIT COMES TO COMFORT

Summarizing the Chapter

In John 14:15–26, Jesus reaches the heart of His message on comfort by extending to disciples of all eras a number of promises, all related to the coming of the Holy Spirit—and all providing every spiritual resource and security believers will ever need to minister effectively for Him.

Getting Started (Choose One)

1. At your job do you work independently or do you rely consistently on input and support from others? Which situation do you prefer? How do you react when others fail to provide the assistance you need?
2. What is the best childhood promise you remember receiving (that was fulfilled)? How did you feel when you received what was promised? What did you wish for as a child that never occurred?

Answering the Questions

1. Understanding what biblical dichotomy will give believers a good grip on the basics of their faith?
2. What is a good one-word definition of true discipleship?

3. What is the literal meaning of the Greek word *parakletos?* How is it translated in most English Bibles?

4. Why is it crucial that we also understand the precise meaning of the Greek adjective *allos* (John 14:16)?

5. Who are the two *paracletes* all Christians have?

6. What is the quality of the unregenerate's perception of spiritual truth?

7. From their reading of the Old Testament, what would the disciples have known of the Holy Spirit's ministry?

8. Concerning their relationship to believers, what do the members of the Trinity have in common?

9. What became clear to Peter and the other apostles on the day of Pentecost?

10. What is the key point of Jesus' answer to Judas' (Thaddaeus') question (John 14:22–24)?

11. Must love and obedience to Christ be perfectly demonstrated in order to be real? Explain, and cite several verses.

12. In whose stead does the Holy Spirit teach? How comprehensive is the "all things" He imparts to believers (see John 14:26)?

13. What was so important about Jesus' promise that the disciples would remember the things He taught them? What Christian doctrine derives from that promise?

Focusing on Prayer

- Thank the Lord for His faithfulness in providing us with His inspired, written Word, which contains all the comfort and resources we need to live for Him.

- Pray that God would daily grant you a greater awareness and appreciation of your union with Him.

Applying the Truth

Memorize and meditate on one or more of the following verses: Matthew 10:19; Romans 8:17; 1 Corinthians 2:9; 1 John 2:1.

CHAPTER 7
THE PEACE OF CHRIST

Summarizing the Chapter

True biblical peace with all its benefits is a gift of Jesus Christ and the Holy Spirit to all believers. It is perfected only as Christians study God's Word and allow the Spirit to direct their hearts and minds away from troubling circumstances and on to the person of Christ.

Getting Started (Choose One)

1. How would you measure your personal "at peace quotient"? Would it be high or low, according to scriptural definitions? Do you have a tendency to let life's difficult circumstances rob you of peace? If so, why do you think that has been true?
2. Do you think diplomatic and political efforts to achieve peace in various regions of the world are worthwhile? Do some conflicts deserve more of those efforts than others? Which ones? Discuss briefly.

Answering the Questions

1. How does the meaning of the Hebrew word *shalom* capture the essence of biblical peace?
2. What two kinds of peace does the New Testament refer to?
3. What is the main result of the gospel message (see 2 Cor. 5:18–19)?

4. Which kind of peace does Jesus mention in John 14:27? What are its main characteristics (see Phil. 4:7)?

5. How did Jesus exhibit perfect experiential peace before Pilate (John 19:10–11)?

6. How meaningful has the expression "world peace" been over the centuries?

7. What is the basic reason people in the world can't find true peace on their own? Give a Bible verse to support your answer.

8. During the time of what prophet was the futility of the world's peace especially evident?

9. In what time frames do people who are experiencing anxiety and turmoil tend to dwell?

10. Why does the analogy of an umpire emerge from Colossians 3:15? What does that suggest about the role of God's peace?

11. What other favorable results, both for the body of Christ and individual Christians, should result from genuine peace (Col. 3:15; 2 Cor. 4:8–11; 11:24–29)?

Focusing on Prayer

- If you are struggling with troublesome circumstances or a difficult trial now, pray that the Lord would give you an extra measure of His peace and help you look away from the problem and toward Him.

- Pray for someone who is facing a complex decision in the near future. Ask that they would allow God's true peace to arbitrate and reveal His will.

Applying the Truth

For the next several months, keep a "peace journal"—either as a separate notebook, or as part of your devotional journal or prayer diary. List the Scripture references from this chapter that were particularly helpful and refer to them when the going gets rough. Keep track of significant anxious times, stressful circumstances, and difficult trials. For each experience, record how well (or poorly) you reacted. Did you have a sense of true peace during and after each situation? Were you successful in looking beyond the circumstances to the peace Christ provides? Write down ways in which you can better maintain a level of biblical peace no matter what's happening around you.

CHAPTER 8
WHAT JESUS' DEATH MEANT TO HIM

Summarizing the Chapter

The disciples anticipated Jesus' death with fear and sorrow, but He looked forward to the Cross with joyful eagerness because of what He would accomplish there: He would experience the Father's exaltation, He would make way for the documentation of more prophecies about His person and work, He would finally and decisively defeat the plans of Satan, and He would demonstrate His obedient love for His Father.

Getting Started (Choose One)

1. Have you and your spouse (or good friend, or close relative) ever anticipated the same event in completely opposite ways? Did you try to persuade the other person to your outlook? What was the biggest lesson you learned after the event was over?
2. Do you think most Christians have the right perspective on death? What would be some major obstacles to keep them from viewing it as God does?

Answering the Questions

1. What were the major elements composing the disciples' faulty outlook of Jesus' upcoming death and departure?
2. Humanly speaking, what is one of the most incomprehensible truths about Christ's incarnation?
3. In John 17:4–5, what was Jesus looking ahead to with joy? How did His divine foreknowledge make that joy more complete (see Heb. 12:2)?
4. What straightforward method did Jesus often use to strengthen the apostles' faith? List some examples of this method.
5. When was the plan of redemption determined?
6. In John 14:30, what does Jesus call Satan?
7. What was Satan's long-term position and strategy regarding the person and mission of Christ?
8. How did the Cross affect the devil's fate? What are the practical implications of this?
9. What does each New Testament mention of Jesus' obedience imply about His relationship to God the Father?

Focusing on Prayer

- Pray that God through His Word would instill in you a greater attitude of humility and servanthood—one that would more closely conform to Jesus' example.
- Thank the Lord that Christ's death and resurrection stripped Satan of any lasting power over us. Ask Him to remind you of this truth whenever you are facing severe temptation.

Applying the Truth

Read *The Murder of Jesus* by John MacArthur, or memorize Philippians 2:6–10.

Study Guide

CHAPTER 9
THE VINE AND THE BRANCHES

Summarizing the Chapter

In John 15:1–6, Jesus uses the metaphor of vine and branches to begin His teaching on spiritual abiding. The vine is Christ, the vinedresser the Father, the fruit-bearing branches are believers, and the fruitless branches are those who merely appear to be genuine believers.

Getting Started (Choose One)

1. Jesus used many agrarian metaphors and analogies when He taught. Would He do that if He were teaching on earth today? What high-tech illustrations might He use? What factors might guide His selection of illustrations?
2. Have you ever known anyone whom you thought was a Christian but discovered later that they "left the faith"? What proved that they were not really a believer? For you, what was the most difficult aspect about that experience?

Answering the Questions

1. What do all the "I am" passages in the Gospel of John underscore about Jesus' identity?
2. How do the characters involved in Christ's upper room discourse make clear the meaning of His metaphors in John 15?
3. How would some Bible students explain Judas' fate? What verses disprove that explanation? What are some basic characteristics of apostates, or false branches?
4. In what way does the Old Testament use a vine as an important metaphor?
5. Give three reasons that Jesus chose the figure of a vine.

6. What inadequate substitutes do professed Christians often rely on for fruitfulness?
7. What is the twofold duty of the Vinedresser (John 15:2)?
8. What is the essence of the Christian life? Does that essence always appear exactly the same?
9. Can someone be attached to the Vine without being a true branch (cite specific references)?
10. What is one of the most frequent and effective ways God prunes us to produce spiritual fruitfulness? What does He use as His pruning knife?

Focusing on Prayer

- Ask the Lord to keep you faithful in His Word every day so that you might abide closer and closer to Christ.
- Pray for a fellow Christian who may be currently undergoing the trials and suffering of God's pruning.

Applying the Truth

Memorize Ephesians 2:10 and seek an opportunity within the next month to do a biblical good work for someone you know. (Try to minister to the person or family with something that is more than just a brief "favor.")

CHAPTER 10
THE BENEFITS OF LIFE IN CHRIST

Summarizing the Chapter

In John 15:7–11, Jesus continues His instruction on abiding and describes what will typify life for the fruitful believer. Genuine spiritual fruitfulness—which includes Christ-like character, gratitude, helpfulness to the needy, pure conduct, and converts—will result in the blessings of answered prayer, abundant life, fullness of joy, and eternal security.

Getting Started (Choose One)

1. When you were a new believer, did you accurately understand spiritual fruitfulness? What was your biggest misconception?
2. It's easy to look to people and things other than Jesus Christ for spiritual success. Which ones of these inadequate alternatives lure you away from the Vine most easily? Why do you think that is?

Answering the Questions

1. What earthly factors are excluded concerning the success or failure of producing spiritual fruit?
2. Approximately how many times does the Bible use the basic word for fruit? Has that frequency of usage meant that most Christians understand the concept?
3. List, along with a relevant Scripture reference, the five main examples of genuine spiritual fruit.
4. How did Jesus and the disciples demonstrate patience in evangelism (see John 4:35–38)?
5. What two conditions are attached to the promise of answered prayer?
6. What is the overriding purpose for the life of every believer? What will each experience if he or she follows that purpose?
7. What kind of attitude causes many Christians not to experience God's joy?
8. Why are some seemingly good branches cast away from the Vine? Can that ever happen to the genuine believer? What does Scripture say?

Focusing on Prayer

- Praise and thank God that He, not us, is the source of our fruit-fulness, and that we have the privilege of abiding in His Son.
- Pray for a friend or relative who may not be experiencing the blessings of abiding in Christ. Ask God to give them a fresher, closer relationship to Christ—or a relationship for the very first time (if they're not saved).

Applying the Truth

Do a more in-depth study on the concept of fruitfulness. Look more carefully (using a study Bible, concordance, commentaries, etc.) at the many references mentioned in that beginning section of this chapter. Prayerfully devise a plan for how you might improve in one area of fruitfulness.

CHAPTER 11
HOW TO BE A FRIEND OF JESUS

Summarizing the Chapter

In John 15:12–16, Jesus shares with His disciples and us these essential characteristics and reassurances concerning intimate friendship with Him: obedience to Him, love for each other, special insight into divine truth, and the call to positions of ministry.

Getting Started (Choose One)

1. Generally speaking, what types of people are easiest to make friends with? What one aspect of friendship do you appreciate the most? Why? Would you ever trade it for some other friendship benefit?

2. Would you enjoy being a special friend, close adviser, or confidant to an important government leader or famous person? What would be the advantages and disadvantages? Discuss briefly.

Answering the Questions

1. What is the Greek word for "servant"? What connotation did it have for the disciples?
2. Who was the only Old Testament figure known as the friend of God?
3. What condition was essential and implied in all the metaphors Jesus used concerning intimate friendship with Him?
4. What should be natural for true friends of Jesus to show toward other Christians?
5. What do we have in common with other believers? What actions and feelings toward them should that motivate?
6. What was the conventional relationship between slaves and masters in biblical times?
7. Which of Jesus' teaching tools was particularly effective in imparting special knowledge to the disciples?
8. In mentioning or discussing the topic of election, the scriptural context always goes beyond what doctrine to include what other concept?
9. In the end, how should a believer's life be different from an unbeliever's?

Focusing on Prayer

- Thank God for His loving and gracious willingness through Christ to make you His friend. Pray that your obedience would deepen that friendship.
- Pray for your church that each member would truly appreciate

the divine truth they've received and realize they are to use it as God-ordained servants of the Lord Jesus.

Applying the Truth

Memorize 1 John 3:16–18 or Romans 5:5.

CHAPTER 12
HATED WITHOUT A CAUSE

Summarizing the Chapter

In John 15:17–25 Christ makes the transition from discussing His love for believers to warning of the world's hatred of them. He alerts the disciples that suffering and persecution will be unavoidable for true Christians because (1) Christians are not of the world, (2) the world hates Christ and the things that pertain to Him, and (3) the world does not know God.

Getting Started (Choose One)

1. What's your opinion of the popular interest in angels in recent years? Does it help or hinder the church's proclamation of the gospel?
2. If it were in your power, what one aspect about the world's system would you eliminate overnight? Why does that one come to mind?

Answering the Questions

1. How and why did the Greek term *martus* evolve in meaning?

2. What does history record about the world's treatment of the apostles after Jesus left?

3. What were Roman citizens required to do annually? What value did that have in the eyes of officials?

4. How did the Apostle John use the word *kosmos* in John 15:19?

5. Throughout history, what has been the most aggressive opponent of real Christianity?

6. What is an inescapable fact of godly living (2 Tim. 3:12)? Why don't more Christians experience it? Give several reasons.

7. What is wrong and unrealistic for churches to expect the world to do regarding its need for salvation?

8. What is the true nature and result of the world's seeming tolerance of Jesus and "spiritual things"?

9. What kind of extreme error and confusion does Satan welcome as much as he does the opportunity to persecute the true church?

10. What is the world's basic approach to religion?

11. What is the real reason people reject the truth about God?

12. Why was the Jews' rejection of Jesus so complete and irreversible? Whose words from the Old Testament did it fulfill?

Focusing on Prayer

- Pray for the pastors and missionaries you know, and all who are ministering the gospel around the world, that God would grant them abundant amounts of strength and courage to withstand opposition and persecution.

- Pray for several people by name from your neighborhood, workplace, or school who are part of the world's darkness and don't know God or the salvation offered through Christ. Ask Him to make you a bolder witness to them.

Applying the Truth

Read and meditate on Nehemiah 1–6. Consider what lessons you can draw in dealing with opposition and staying with the task God has given you.

Additional Books in "The Bible for Life" series

What the Bible Says About Parenting

More than ever, Christians need to know what the Bible teaches about parenting. Pastor/teacher John MacArthur presents time-proven principles of biblical parenting clearly and carefully to help parents make sense of their duties before God and to bring up their children in the ways of the Lord.

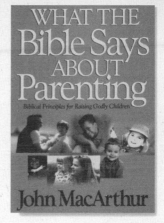

Whose Money Is It Anyway?

In this no-nonsense, practical book, renowned Bible scholar John MacArthur cuts through popular opinion to the core of what the Bible says about money and materialism. Discussing the topics of instant gratification, giving, and success, MacArthur challenges readers to loosen their grip on their purse strings and instead turn their focus towards a richer relationship with God.

Why Government Can't Save You

Renowned pastor and author John MacArthur takes a look at the political responsibilities of a Christian by delving into what the Bible says about a Christian's responsibility toward authority, the biblical purposes of government, and how to support our governmental leaders. Using Paul's example before worldly authorities and Jesus' lessons to Peter, MacArthur challenges Christians to remember our true status as we act responsibly in matters of politics.

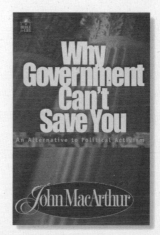

WORD PUBLISHING
www.wordpublishing.com

Additional Releases from John MacArthur

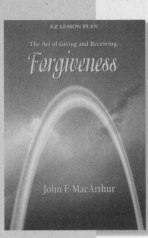

Forgiveness EZ Lesson Plan

In this three-session EZ Lesson Plan, noted biblical scholar John MacArthur provides an insightful look at forgiveness. MacArthur not only reminds us that we are called to grant forgiveness to those who sin against us, but he also teaches the importance of learning to accept the forgiveness of others.

The Gospel According to the Apostles

John MacArthur takes a solid look at some of the most divisive faith issues in evangelical circles today. Presenting a thorough discussion of the "lordship salvation," he addresses such issues as assurance of salvation, righteousness and imperfection, "cheap grace," and the importance of obedience in the Christian life.

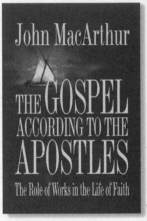

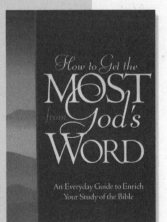

How to Get the Most From God's Word

From one of today's most popular Bible speakers, you can learn to effectively apply Bible teachings and principles to your own life. This practical Bible study companion cuts to the heart of God's Word and shows you how to do the same.

Introduction to Biblical Counseling

Solid theological foundations of biblical counseling are clearly presented in contrast to humanistic and secular theories of psychological counseling. A practical, proactive, and relevant book for students, church leaders, and lay people. This collection of writers represents some of America's leading biblical teachers and counselors.

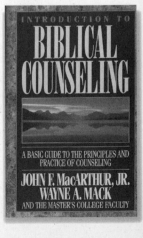

WORD PUBLISHING

www.wordpublishing.com

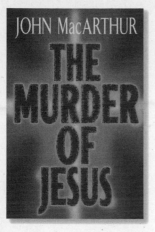

The Murder of Jesus
Two thousand years ago, an unprecedented conspiracy of injustice, cruelty, and religious and political interests sentenced a man guilty of no crimes to the most barbaric method of execution ever devised. Piecing together the narrative from the perspective of the participants, MacArthur relives the most awesome injustice in the history of man and the unparalleled triumph of the sovereignty of God.

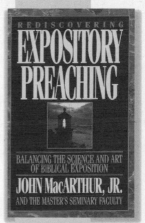

Rediscovering Expository Preaching
John MacArthur and his colleagues at The Master's Seminary offer a definitive manual on "rightly dividing the Word of truth" for today's congregations. With insight and clarity, they examine the four steps of Bible exposition, emphasizing the role of study and prayer in sermon preparation.

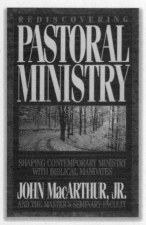

Rediscovering Pastoral Ministry
Encouraging, insightful and challenging, *Rediscovering Pastoral Ministry* is designed for a new generation of shepherds who seek to lead with the passion of the apostles. Written by MacArthur and his colleagues at The Master's Seminary, this guide outlines the biblical priorities essential to effective ministry.

The Vanishing Conscience
In this compelling book, MacArthur sounds a wake-up call for Christians to confront society's flight from moral responsibility and recognize sin for what it is. In doing so, he says, we can move from living a life of blame and denial to one of true peace and freedom.

🍷 WORD PUBLISHING
www.wordpublishing.com

The MacArthur Bible Collection
John MacArthur, General Editor

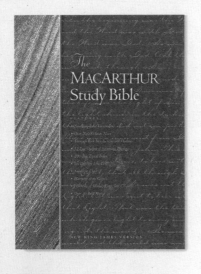

The MacArthur Study Bible

From the moment you pick it up, you'll know it's a classic. Featuring the word-for-word accuracy of the New King James Version, *The MacArthur Study Bible* is perfect for serious study. Pastor/teacher John MacArthur has compiled more than 20,000 study notes, a 200-page topical index, and numerous charts, maps, outlines, and articles to create *The MacArthur Study Bible*. This Bible has been crafted with the finest materials in a variety of handsome bindings, including hardcover and indexed bonded leather. Winner of "The 1998 Study Bible of the Year Award."

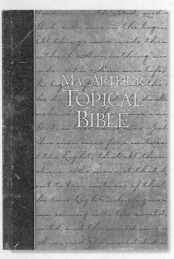

The MacArthur Topical Bible

In the excellent tradition of *Nave's Topical Bible,* this newly created reference book incorporates thousands of topics and ideas, both traditional and contemporary, for believers today and in the new millennium. Carefully researched and prepared by Dr. John MacArthur and the faculty of Masters Seminary, *The MacArthur Topical Bible* will quickly become the reference of choice for all serious Bible students. Using the New King James translation, this Bible is arranged alphabetically by topic and is completely cross-referenced. This exhaustive resource is an indispensible tool for the topical study of God's Word.

WORD PUBLISHING
www.wordpublishing.com

The MacArthur Bible Studies

Ruth & Esther, Daniel, John, Acts, Galatians, 1 & 2 Peter, Ephesians, Mark, 1 Samuel, & Romans

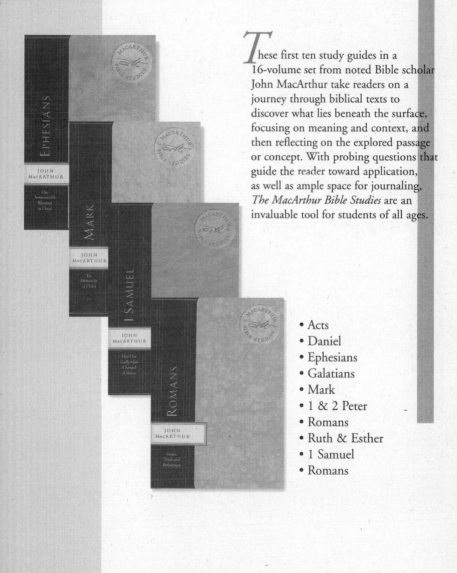

These first ten study guides in a 16-volume set from noted Bible scholar John MacArthur take readers on a journey through biblical texts to discover what lies beneath the surface, focusing on meaning and context, and then reflecting on the explored passage or concept. With probing questions that guide the reader toward application, as well as ample space for journaling, *The MacArthur Bible Studies* are an invaluable tool for students of all ages.

- Acts
- Daniel
- Ephesians
- Galatians
- Mark
- 1 & 2 Peter
- Romans
- Ruth & Esther
- 1 Samuel
- Romans

W WORD PUBLISHING
www.wordpublishing.com